To Doris,

May Dads' love fill well
your days with Joy

I Cor. 13

GOD DRIVES
A PICKUP TRUCK

Amazing Grace - Text: John Newton; John P. Rees, stanza 5. Music: Traditional American melody from Carrell and Clayton's *Virginia Harmony,* 1831

Love Lifted Me - Text: James Rowe. Music: Howard E. Smith
© 1912, Renewal 1940 by Mrs. Howard Smith. Assigned to Singspiration (ASCAP), Div. of Zondervan Corp. All rights reserved. Used by permission.

General Sources:
Herzstein, R.E., *et al., The Nazis.* Alexandria, Va: Time-Life, 1980
Keegan, John, *The Second World War.* New York: Viking, 1989
Manchester, William, *The Glory and the Dream: A Narrative History of America 1932-1972.* Boston: Little Brown Company, 1974
Wernick, Robert, *et al., Blitzkrieg.* New York: Time-Life, 1976

Cover Illustration:
Debbie Fanning © 1999
Cover illustrator, Debbie Fanning, is a freelance artist living in San Antonio.

Editor:
Martha Fanning

Cover Design:
Andrea Hernandez

Copy Editors:
Ann Elrod, Stanley Weaver, Wende Whitus

Published by:
LifeWorks Publishing
7967 Turf Paradise Lane
Fair Oaks Ranch, TX 78015
210-698-2758 Fax: 210-698-9158

Printed and bound in the United States of America by:
Millennia Graphics, Colorado Springs, CO

ISBN 0-9621073-6-0

Buy this book! You will be cheered, helped and inspired. And you will learn why Buckner Fanning has become one of America's most admired preachers and beloved pastors.

Howard Butt, Jr.
President, H.E. Butt and Laity Lodge Foundations
Vice Chairman, Board of H.E. Butt Grocery Company

Buckner Fanning is one of the great preachers of our time because he is a master storyteller. Like the Bible, this book is full of stories, stories that will help you discover how much God loves you.

Bruce Larson
Pastor, author and conference speaker

In the same spirit of the Gospels, Buckner Fanning uses the very ordinary stories of life to bring out the extraordinary love of God. Beyond this, they are an inspiration for people of any faith.

Virgil Elizondo
Director of Program Development of Catholic Television
and former Rector, San Fernando Cathedral, San Antonio

Buckner Fanning's life is an open book; so are his writings. From stories of broken vases in his mother's living room to broken hearts in war-torn Nagasaki you will sense his pathos, his wisdom, and his redemptive hope.

Bruce McIver
Pastor, author and conference speaker

DEDICATION

This book is dedicated to Martha, my loving wife of over fifty years, who has made our home a heaven on earth, and who has been indispensable in every good thing that has happened in our lives together.

To our three children Michael, Stephen and Lisa, who have been an incomparable joy to my life; and to their wonderful, loving partners in Christian marriage, Harriet, Debbie and George Pilgrim, all of whom I love as my own.

To four Fanning grandchildren — Avery, Julia, Meagan and Michael, Jr. — whom I love beyond words to express, and who bring indescribable joy and inspiration to my life.

To Trinity Baptist Church in San Antonio — the most loving, grace-filled congregation on the earth — a wonderful, exciting fellowship that epitomizes unconditional love for all mankind.

My Deep Gratitude

... to Judy Pearson, who has gone to be with the Lord. She was my devoted personal secretary for more than 14 years and typed the original manuscript.

... and to Ann Elrod, for her diligence in copy editing and fact checking.

Contents

PREFACE

Remember the film, *Fried Green Tomatoes?* In one of the most poignant scenes, the irrepressible Idgie consoled the brokenhearted son of her closest friend who was dying of cancer. Idgie said to the grieving child, "There are a lot of angels masquerading around this planet as people and your mother is one of them."

How true! Our planet is blessed with thousands of masquerading angels. Many of these angels — God's instruments — have blessed my life with His music and kept me in tune with His plans for me.

God's angels are everywhere! Our insensitivity to them — our tone deafness, if you will — robs us of the rich music they can bring to our lives. When we become receptive to God's music, we will be amazed and comforted by the angels He uses to communicate with us.

In the *Old Testament,* God provided rainbows, rocks, donkeys, and burning bushes to deliver divine messages. Nowadays, He uses pickup trucks, cookies, and broken vases to show His love for us. The instruments have changed, the music remains the same.

In 1857 — more than a century before Idgie's character appeared on screen — the ethereal poet, Elizabeth Barrett Browning, wrote:

> *Earth's crammed with Heaven*
> *And every bush afire with God;*
> *But only he who sees takes off his shoes,*
> *The rest stand or sit around it*
> *and pluck blackberries.*

I confess. I've spent time plucking (and eating) blackberries. We all have. They taste so good! The delicious blackberries can distract us from the "bush afire with God." And earthly desserts can cause us to miss the music of masquerading angels. The good can often be the enemy of the best.

Idgie and Elizabeth restate what God has written: "Do not forget to entertain strangers, for by so doing some people have entertained angels without knowing it." (*Hebrews 13:2*). Reading God's word reminds us to respond to "the bush afire with God" and reach out to masquerading angels.

Past experiences make me mindful of the masquerading angels in the mundane. I often pray: "Dear God, keep my spiritual eyes and ears open to the subtle and powerful expressions of Your love. May I see, hear, and feel Your grace revealed in unexpected places and unlikely people."

I've been blessed by many a bush "afire with God" and encountered numerous masquerading angels who have touched and transformed my life. This book shares some of these encounters.

I pray the words written here will enable you to recognize the angels in your life. I hope these pages help you laugh a little, think some, appreciate more, and, perhaps, shed a tear or two. May you be inspired to see the angels abounding in your world and be set afire by the music of the Lord.

DR. BUCKNER FANNING
OCTOBER, 1999

THE BROKEN VASE

My wonderful Christian mother — a patient, intelligent, and understanding woman who deeply loved the Lord, her family and her church — had strong convictions as to what was right and what was wrong. Looking back on those years, I am now thankful for her ideals. Of course, that's not to say I always agreed with her at the time, for I didn't, but I now thank God for her and her sensible, logical convictions.

On the major moral issues facing us all, my mother was both firm and loving in her attitude. Firm and loving! What a divine combination.

Even though time's passage proved my mother correct on almost all of her convictions, there were some rules that galled me at the time. One regulation, in particular, caused me considerable consternation. I didn't feel this commandment was a major moral issue. My mother felt otherwise.

This "Thou Shalt Not," spoken from her personal Mt. Sinai, had to do with throwing a baseball in the house. "Thou Shalt Not Throw a Baseball in the House" failed to make Moses' top ten, but it was definitely among the top fifteen on mother's list, and we knew it!

Her protective pronouncement, "Thou Shalt Not Throw a Baseball in the House" rolled like thunder from on high and although the commandment nettled my brother, Bob, and me, we never for a moment doubted nor questioned the seriousness of our mother's ultimatum. Never!

My mother had collected some beautiful antiques across many years, antiques for which she had saved and sacrificed. These treasured antiques occupied a prominent place in our home.

Two of her antiques were prized above all others. One was a three legged chair. I had no appreciation for that chair because its three legs made it look weird, twisted and deformed. Every time I looked at that chair, I thought of three-horned cows, birds with three heads, or some other freak animal seen at carnival side shows. Didn't my mother know that every orthodox chair had four legs? Of what use could a three-legged chair be to anyone? Despite the chair's freakish appearance, my mother treasured it. Perhaps, I thought, she felt sorry for the poor, deformed chair.

Another strange thing about that chair — my mother never allowed anyone to sit in it. Ever! You were supposed to just stand there breathlessly admiring it as "a thing of beauty and joy forever." This added to my suspicion of that chair.

Many years later, following the death of our parents, Bob and I, along with our wives, Carolyn and Martha, divided the possessions of our parents, and — you guessed it — I received the chair, proving once again God's sense of humor!

Where does that chair sit today? You're right. In our living room. And you know something else? We never allow anyone to sit in it. Nobody! You only are permitted to gaze at it with breathless appreciation. My prejudice about the "deformed chair" has been transformed to admiration. I, like, my mother before me, treasure that chair.

Early parental influence is an unappreciated, powerful force that can be used for shaping good or bad behavior. The folk proverb "the fruit seldom falls very far from the tree" continues to ring true. Sometimes the fruit produces rancid, bitter, poisonous crops; at other times the fruit yields a bountiful harvest.

If my mother's attitude subtly transformed my opinion regarding a weird, misshapen, useless three legged chair, just imagine how she shaped my outlook on more vital issues. As parents and grandparents we must be careful to make certain that the fruit of our influence results in exemplary crops.

Occupying the other corner of our living room was my mother's "prize antique," a beautiful, stately, hand-painted antique vase about two feet tall with a brass base and a porcelain top with a brass handle. The vase resided in the most prominent corner of the living room like a queen on a throne.

One rainy, dreary day in Dallas, my brother, Bob, and I stood at the back door of our home forlornly watching the pouring rain spoil our Saturday. With baseball gloves in hand and our Louisville Slugger leaning against the near wall, we dawdled, our noses pressed close to the screen door, wishing for the torrent to turn into a trickle.

The harder we wished, the more thunderous the rain fell. Bob began beating in his baseball glove, keeping vigorous time with the "tat, tat, tat" of the torrential rain. Bob's rhythmic pounding, combined with my need to warm-up, caused my arm to begin twitching, ever so slightly.

As I shook my arm to relieve the twitch, I felt a powerful pressure rising from my inner being. This irresistible impulse most likely stemmed from my being the pitcher on our neighborhood baseball team. I gently rolled the pearly Rawling's baseball in my right palm caressing the tightly woven red stitching as I changed grips from fastball, to curve, to change-up. I needed to warm-up to be ready to pitch when the rain stopped. My resistance against the Fifteenth Commandment began to erode. When Bob declared "I would give anything if we could toss your new ball a few times," my moral power completely dissolved.

A series of small events transformed me into an animal, a creature without civility. My impulses completely controlled me. My reasoning became distorted.

I replied to Bob, "I really don't think mother would mind a whole lot if we threw a few careful pitches in the living room. She's understanding. She knows it's raining. I bet she's feeling sorry for us. I think she would let us throw the ball a little bit in the living room, don't you?"

Bob quickly concurred, "Let's try it."

(I must pause at this point to tell you that today my brother, Robert A. Fanning, is an extremely successful attorney in Dallas. The mystifying point in this entire story is that Bob now receives large fees for giving advice like that!)

We moved quietly into the living room to test our theory with two or three well controlled tosses. When we heard no commandments from mother who was cooking supper in the kitchen, our throws began to heat-up. After all, every boy knows that since the invention of doors, mothers have been capable of hearing infinitesimal sounds through any closed door. Because the closed door between the kitchen and living room acted as megaphone for mother, her silence confirmed our belief that she felt empathy for our being house bound.

Soon, Bob took the "catcher's" position at the end of the living room with the deformed chair on his left and the beautiful vase on his right. I pitched from the opposite end of the living room, about 15 feet from where mother was working.

Bob whispered, "What are you going to throw?"

"A fast ball" I whispered back.

I wish you could have seen the pitch! It was magnificent! Nolan Ryan never threw a better one. The ball, nearly ripping the glove off Bob's hand, hit his catcher's mitt like an explosion! Pow!

We froze. Our mother heard the concussion — she had to have heard it — but she continued preparing supper, not saying a word. We smiled knowingly at one another as if to say, "We've got it made."

I grooved a few more fast balls right down the middle and then said; "Bob, I think I'm going to try a curve ball — some of my breaking stuff."

Little did I know how literally true my prediction would be. I wound up and stretched, preparing to throw the curve ball to end all curve balls.

You never saw such a curve, and neither had my brother. He leaped for the ball, missing the toss by a mile. Give him credit for a noble effort, but the wild pitch zoomed past him, smashing the vase into a thousand pieces. My noble brother, the successful attorney, took off out the back door and disappeared into the pouring rain.

I ran over to the scene of the crime to examine the evidence and when I saw the sickening sight my first thought was, "maybe she didn't hear the explosion." She heard it. She couldn't help but hear it. The cacophony sounded like an airplane crashing.

I thought of gluing the shattered pieces together with model airplane epoxy, but the vase was too fragmented for that idea to work. I could never restore the original beauty of the vase. Besides, the sin had been committed. Mother had heard the crash. A cover-up would fail.

I fully expected her to show up at the scene of the crime any minute, but she didn't. She just kept right on working in the kitchen. I stood there beside what was left of the vase and asked myself, "What in the world have you done?"

I had broken my mother's prize antique. I couldn't plead innocence or ignorance. I knew better. She'd told me a thousand times not to throw the baseball in the house, but I had broken her commandment — intentionally. At that moment, I would have given anything if the earth had just opened up and swallowed me.

Mother continued preparing supper as though nothing had happened. I didn't know what to do. Finally, I collected enough courage to quietly walk into the kitchen. My mother was working at the sink, her back toward me. She knew I'd come into the room, but she didn't turn around or say a word. I stood there for what seemed like an eternity with my heart pounding and my mouth as dry as the Sahara Desert.

Suddenly, out of the depths of my soul I said: "Mother, I'm real sorry. I broke your vase and I'm sorry. I really am."

She continued working for a few moments and then stopped, slowly turned, and looked straight at me for a few seconds without saying a word. And then ... she smiled. That's all! She just smiled and without a word returned to preparing supper.

I stood there for a few moments, stunned. I didn't know what to do or to say. I just stood there. Finally, I walked out of the kitchen in a daze of bewilderment and bumped into my rain-soaked brother who had garnered enough courage to return.

Seeing the dazed look on my face, he excitedly asked, "What happened?"

All I could do was stammer, "Bob, I don't know what happened, but I want to tell you something. I'm never going to throw the baseball in the house again. Never."

I never threw the baseball in the house again. Just as important, I listened to my mother with more respect thereafter.

I had been forgiven. I had received grace — amazing grace — and the power of my mother's forgiving grace had completely changed my attitude and my actions.

All the "Thou shalt nots" and all the "Don'ts," failed to work. Prohibitions never have, and never will work. All the religion, all the laws and commandments and Biblical warnings, as truthful as they may be, cannot change attitudes and desires. Of course, they may temporarily alter behavior out of fear of punishment or hope of gain, but they are powerless to change desires — powerless to change the heart.

Religious laws and regulations can point the direction, but they cannot provide the energy to make the trip. The law is like a road map. If we have no fuel — no love — in the tank we're not going anywhere! Love provides the energy to follow the road map's direction.

The fuel necessary for the trip is the energizing power of love produced by forgiveness — the most powerful source of love in the world! The power to change the human heart, and the power to change the world, is not law, but love! Not coercion, but compassion!

Years passed. I grew up, graduated from high school in 1943 and went into the Marine Corps for three-and-a-half years. I returned home in August, 1946. Then, on August 31, 1946 in an outdoor revival service in Dallas, something clicked inside me.

I told the Lord in words strangely similar to the words I'd spoken in the kitchen many years earlier: "I'm sorry, Lord. I'm really sorry. I knew your commandments and I broke them. I knew better, but I did wrong anyway. I've tried to fix everything up — to glue my life all back together with promises and resolutions, but the glue doesn't hold."

Something happened to me that hot August night strangely similar to what happened in the kitchen many years before. An event that changed my life. God smiled at me. He'd forgiven me. My world was suddenly expanded.

But there's more. I entered Baylor University in the fall of 1946 and shortly after began preaching in "Youth Revivals" throughout the state. I felt God had called me into the ministry. Christmas came and all the family gathered together at our home in Dallas to celebrate. This was my first Christmas home after three-and-a-half years away spent in military service.

As always, my mother gave me a gift. The package was large. As I carefully opened the gift, I saw the vase! The resurrected vase! A vase more lovely than the original! I cried and I cry now as I think and write about the experience.

In the same room where I had broken the original vase, a new vase had come to life, and a new Buckner had been created — not perfect, not sinless, but new, with new desires and new directions.

Unknown to anyone, my mother, for over five years, had searched for a replacement for that broken vase — a replacement that would perfectly fit the brass fittings — the only survivors of the shattered vase. She found an exquisite hand-painted antique vase, more attractive than the original, and had it mounted with the fittings from the old vase.

Today, the resurrected vase occupies a prominent place in our home. I see it every day. Every time I pass that vase, I am reminded of the smile of God and the transforming power of forgiveness. I recall once again of what it means to receive grace, to be forgiven.

As I write these words, I smile again. I smile as I think of my loving mother who gave me my first lesson in grace and who was for me an angel masquerading as a human being.

Sacrificial love is what the cross of Christ is all about. That empty cross we see on so many occasions is God's symbolic reminder to all of us that we are forgiven by His grace. Through His love, He restores what our disobedience has broken. With a warm smile on His loving face, He hands us the gift of Himself! The gift of forgiveness! The gift of love! The most powerful force in the world.

AMAZING GRACE: REFLECTIONS ON THE BROKEN VASE

As I reflect on my life's convolutions, the example established by a broken vase became my defining moment. My moral journey — beginning with a sickening shatter — traversed through sunrises and sunsets, steep slopes, slips and slides into shadowed valleys, and sensational summits, as the radiant never-ending light, the light of forgiving love and transforming grace, summoned me always forward.

This remarkable experience enabled me to comprehend — in the head and in the heart — the Bible's declaration that, "God is love." God is more than loving; He possesses more than the capacity to love: God *is* love! Love is the intrinsic nature of God. God is creator — a loving creator. God is judge — a loving judge.

The law, given by a loving God, makes life better and happier for us all. The law of God, contrary to destroying joy, gives all of us the opportunity for an abundant life! The law of God improves life for everyone.

Is the moral law true because God gave us rules for living, or did God give the commandments because they are true? Both interpretations are correct.

Imagine that God never gave the moral law. Or, pretend that God does not exist. Even without God, wouldn't life be better without murder, stealing, lying, sexual unfaithfulness or disrespect for parents? Yes. All would agree that life would be better in a world filled with righteous living. What a wonderful world that would be!

Because God desires for all of us to have a joyful and peaceful life, God created His law — a law that even if God failed to exist would give us an abundant life. God gave us the law — a beneficial law. The law of God was given to help produce "the good life."

Instead of attempting to ruin our "party," God wants to guide our lives so that we can have a grand celebration on earth and a heavenly celebration forever.

Breaking God's law brings a heavy penalty. These consequences are not meant to punish, but to teach. God's purposes are always redemptive, not punitive. God wants us to learn that His law is good. God never punishes. If we ask with a humble and contrite heart, God always forgives.

Touching a hot stove brings burning pain. Breaking God's Law brings, sooner or later, heart pain. When we ask for forgiveness, God grants our request. The consequences for breaking His law, remain.

Your child touches a hot stove, receives a burn, and asks for your forgiveness because you had warned your child that hot stoves burn. Although you forgive the child for disobedience, the child's hand remains burned. How many times the child touches the hot stove depends on the child's mental intelligence.

Likewise, how many times we break God's law depends on our spiritual intelligence. Just as God's forgiveness remains constant, the consequences of breaking His law persist. Eventually most of us learn that God's law is good. Those who fail to learn will continue to suffer the consequences of God's law.

I vividly remember disciplining my children when, against my words of caution, they continued riding their tricycles in the street. Their tear-filled, wide eyes looked up at me with a mixture of anger and surprise because I punished them. I knew they thought the street was made for kids on tricycles. They also knew I wanted them to have fun, but because I could see potential consequences beyond their knowledge, I was compelled to punish them for their own protection. I knew that, in time, they would realize my discipline was an act of painful love, not an act of anger.

Therefore, if I, a sinful human being, have that kind of love for my children, how much more love does our heavenly Father have for all His children!

Since the law was and is an expression of God's great love for mankind, sin is not so much breaking God's law as it is breaking God's heart. My heart hurt when I punished my children for riding their tricycles in the street, but I was willing to suffer their displeasure, even their anger, because I loved them more than life itself! By breaking my rules my children were potentially breaking my heart. This is why I believe sin is more than breaking God's law; sin also breaks God's heart.

And now this question arises: How can we make atonement for a broken heart? We know how to make atonement for a broken law. We pay the penalty the law demands, and after that the law has no further claim upon us. But how do we make atonement for a broken heart?

Suppose I'm driving down the street, paying only casual attention to my speed, when suddenly, a child runs from behind a parked car and I hit and kill the child. I am totally devastated. That accident would be absolutely the worst thing that could ever happen to me.

Of course, I had not been drinking. Nor had I run a stop sign or red light. I may have been slightly exceeding the speed limit by a mile or two per hour, or perhaps I failed to "maintain a proper look-out." Whatever the mitigating circumstances might be, I am emotionally shattered by what I've done.

In the courtroom I tell the judge, "I'm guilty. I'm guilty, and I want you to give me the full penalty of the law." Imagine the judge sentences me to three years in jail and a $5,000 fine. I go to jail and pay the fine.

As soon as I'm released, I go to the home of the little child whom I had accidentally killed and knock on the door. The mother of the child comes to the door, and I say, "You will be pleased and satisfied to know that I have been to jail for three years and paid a $5,000 fine and therefore I know that everything between us is all right. Do you agree?"

The mother looks at me like she thinks I'm insane. I can imagine that the mother is saying to herself, "Is this man so demented as to believe that simply because he's been in jail and paid a fine, my heart no longer breaks? Does this man's distorted thinking make him feel that because he has paid the penalty the law demands, his actions will now fill the empty chair at our breakfast table every morning? Does he feel that paying the penalty of the law will bring back the ringing laughter in our home? This man is crazy."

She closes the door, and I walk away.

I begin to ask myself, "What must I do to overcome her reluctance and earn her forgiveness?"

I decide to demonstrate my penitence by crawling up and down the sidewalk in front of her house on my knees. I do this hour after hour while praying, crying and begging for forgiveness. I continue until my knees are bloody and my body is emaciated. Then I struggle up to the door and once again I ask, "Does this satisfy you? Can you now forgive me? I've been in jail. I've paid a fine. I've suffered physically. I've knelt, prayed and cried penitently appealing for your forgiveness."

She is unmoved.

I stand there stunned. What can I do? Nothing. There is absolutely nothing I can do to earn forgiveness and experience a restoration of a relationship between myself and the mother. There is no physical or spiritual act I can perform to earn her forgiveness. There is absolutely nothing I can do. Forgiveness must begin with the mother. Forgiveness, and the restoration of a relationship, must begin with her!

Originating within the heart of the mother must be a spirit of love and forgiveness that reaches out to me and says, "Whether you go to jail, pay a fine, pray, cry and ask for forgiveness or not makes no difference to me. I choose to forgive you whether you go to jail or not; whether you pray and cry or not, whether you ask for forgiveness or not. I forgive you because I love you."

Forgiveness must begin with the one whose heart I've broken, not whose law I have broken. And that is exactly what Jesus Christ has done! He died for our sins because He loved us and rose from the grave to say, "You are forgiven — whether you feel penitent or not; whether you are remorseful or not; whether you ask for forgiveness or not; whether you go to the jail of depression or not. I forgive you, because I love you!"

No wonder when we sing *Amazing Grace,* we are amazed to know that Jesus has forgiven our sins and we can "Go in peace" (*Luke 7:50*). When we experience God's forgiveness we sing, with awe, the words from Charles H. Gabriel's stirring hymn: "I Stand Amazed in the Presence" of Jesus the Nazarene and wonder how He could love me — "a sinner, condemned and unclean. How marvelous. How wonderful."

For by grace you have been saved, through faith —

and that is not from yourselves,
it is the gift of God —
not of works, so that no one can boast.

(Eph. 2:8-9)

Thank God for the shattered vase. Thank God for my mother's response. Thank God for His law. Thank God for His amazing grace.

ANGELS REVISITED

Life, dramatically changed by inscrutable events beyond our control, becomes most clear retrospectively. On the morning of August 6, 1945, the B-29, *Enola Gay*, dropped, over Hiroshima, the uranium 235 version of the atomic bomb; a few hours later, while 78,000 people lay dead or dying in the ruins, the United States called on the Japanese to surrender. No word being received, another B-29, on August 9, 1945, released the second atomic bomb over the city of Nagasaki, destroying 35,000 lives. A few days later, as a Private First Class in the Sixth Regiment of the Second Marine Division, I, with the other Marine occupational forces, marched into the scorched and still flaming city of Nagasaki, an experience made more significant with each maturing year.

The phrase, "Remember Pearl Harbor," resounds with vivid recollections. After church, Sunday, December 7th, 1941, my mother, father, Bob and I visited the home of my parent's friends, Mr. and Mrs. Ben Ball and their children. While waiting for lunch to be served, I, along with the other boys, tossed the football in the back yard. Suddenly, in a voice more urgent than her usual Sunday dinner announcement, my mother called from the back door, "Everybody come quickly! You must listen to what's happening!"

Bob and I sat on the floor, listening to the radio announcements of the Japanese attack on Pearl Harbor, a place that I failed to recognize from my geography studies; nor did I comprehend, at fifteen years of age, how dramatically the raid would change my life and alter history. An entire generation had been "called in from play."

The next day, some older friends of mine quit high school to join the Army. A number of those carefree boys, whom I'd admired for their athletic grace, never again enjoyed running full tilt in the thick, Texas turf of autumn's field but, instead, fell, mortally wounded, on the beaches of Normandy, or suffered grievous wounds in France, Italy, or the Pacific atolls.

Fifteen months after the day of infamy, on my 17th birthday, with my father at my side, I enlisted in the United States Marine Corps. After graduation from high school in May, I left for active duty. The next three-and-a-half years, I spent in the Marine Corps where I was later assigned to the Second Marine Division on Saipan, after a brief period on the island of Guam.

Those born since World War II fail to comprehend the depth of patriotic devotion in America during the war years. Every American became deeply committed to rid the world of the despotism and destruction created by Hitler, Mussolini, and Hirohito. Those granted deferment, because of age or sex, from active military duty, contributed on the home front by any method available — planting victory gardens, manufacturing war materials, rationing commodities — to protect freedom and justice around the world.

Our country's younger generations, pleased with their cost-efficient Japanese products, have little empathy for the profound loathing World War II Americans possessed for Japan's evil empire. Each passing war year, with escalating reports of Japanese atrocities and the battle deaths of friends, the devotion to the tyrant's defeat deepened.

A thoroughly and effectively trained Marine, I never wavered in my love for country and my commitment to the Corps. The Corps, for which I will be forever grateful, instilled in me a sense of responsibility, discipline, patriotism, and devotion. The Marine

Corps motto, *Semper Fidelis* — Always Faithful — became a noble principle, a principle of faithfulness to God, to others and to myself that remains, to this day, a primary commitment of my life.

When we received rumors, or in Marine Corps lingo, "scuttle butt," that a uniquely powerful bomb — a secret weapon — had ended the war, our excitement about peace fueled the expectation that we would return home soon. We'd never heard the term "atomic bomb," but, a few days later, seeing the noisome obliteration wrought by a nuclear weapon, made me then, as now, repeat Oppenheimer's reminder from *Bhagavad-Gita* — "I am become Death, the shatterer of worlds."

After the peace treaty ending the war with Japan was signed on September 2, 1945, in Tokyo Bay, the Second Marine Division landed in Nagasaki where we lived for many months doing occupational duty. What I saw there confounded and confused me. The destructive devastation rendered by the bomb to both people and property defies description. Thousands of wounded Japanese bore horrible scars, both internally and externally, that would remain with them for their lifetime. Many of the injured children knew less about the cause and events of World War II than my young children knew, later, about Vietnam.

During the months in Nagasaki, something began to change inside me. The juxtaposition of two emotions, love and hate, created by the war and the results of the atomic bomb, precipitated a chain reaction in my soul that ultimately produced a different kind of "explosion" in my life. The sympathy and compassion I felt for all the innocent people tormented by the agony of war's destructiveness, gradually softened my hatred for the Japanese warriors and war lords.

When I left home to join the Marines, my Christian mother gave me a Bible. That Bible, I'm ashamed to report, remained in the bottom of my duffel bag, unopened and unread, for many months. Private First Class Buckner Fanning, "a Marine-made man," had no need for church either.

Although a professing Christian, I failed to take my dedication to the Lord seriously. Even though I believed in being "always faithful" to the Marine Corps and my fellow Marines, I was unfaithful to the Lord. Gradually, however, my conflicting emotions about the Japanese engendered a need for a closer relationship with God. My troubled spirit longed for worship.

After a few months, I found my way to a small Japanese Methodist church. I can't remember how I first heard about the church or exactly when I started attending. I do recall, however, the comfort I gained from church attendance even though I couldn't understand the Japanese sermon or hymns.

Early on Sunday mornings, I would help the pastor set up the chairs in a borrowed building they were using, because their church had been destroyed by our bomb. After distributing the hymnals, I sat in the back of the tiny room, reading the Bible as the Japanese service progressed. Although I failed to understand the Japanese words, I began hearing a "still small voice" that needs no translation. God whispered His love for me and those with whom I worshipped. At the conclusion of each service, I would participate in the Lord's Supper, sharing bread and wine with the rest of the congregation in remembrance of Christ's love for us all.

This small band of Christians, perhaps no more than fifty Japanese, communicated to me in the universal language of love, that they, whose lives had been unmercifully altered by my country's bomb, accepted me as a Christian brother. As we shared communion together, an act of Christian love, the congregation implied that, despite war, hatred, suffering and death — despite racial, national and cultural differences — I was accepted as their brother in Christ. Welcomed as a member of the "family of God" in their church, I learned from those suffering Japanese people that love transcends all human, political, racial, national and ideological differences. In Christ we — all of us — are "One!"

The traumatic experiences of seeing first-hand the devastation of the atomic bomb at Nagasaki, and my acceptance in a loving Methodist church there, became a powerful experience that God used to change my life. Who could have imagined that God could use something as terrible as an atomic bomb to change a person's life? Yet, He did. Yes — He really does "work all things together for good."

After the war, God continued working in my life by slowly changing my attitudes and actions. I felt a growing impression that God was calling me into the ministry. The same year I graduated from Baylor University, 1949, God led me to marry a young, Southern Methodist University beauty, who, in my mind, is the finest, most beautiful, loving and talented woman in the world — Martha Howell.

Martha, a deeply devoted Christian, was one among many who encouraged me in my sense of "calling" to God's service. I attended New Orleans Baptist Theological Seminary for two years and then spent two more years studying at Southwestern Theological Seminary from where I graduated. For ten years, Martha, an outstanding soloist, and I traveled throughout much of America conducting hundreds of evangelistic crusades.

In 1959, I was called to be the pastor of the Trinity Baptist Church in San Antonio, Texas. God's grace continued exploding in my life.

Throughout those years in evangelism there were many "masquerading angels" who touched and directed our lives. Looking back, I see their powerful influence upon my life and my work. Three of the greatest experiences to ever occur in my life were the births of our three children — Mike, Steve and Lisa. God alone knows how much I loved them from the day of their birth to now.

In 1975, our family experienced a startling surprise! I unexpectedly received an invitation from the Nagasaki Baptist church, and from the Mayor of Nagasaki, to return to their city to speak for 10 days, commemorating the 30th anniversary of the dropping of the atomic bomb. I was stunned, humbled and even a little frightened by the invitation. What would I say? And do?

We believed God wanted us to go. Martha and I, our three children, and twenty-five people from Trinity participated in this historic event. People from our church met with their vocational counterparts in Japan, endeavoring to show that building bridges of Christian love could bring nations together who had formerly hated and battled one another.

Engineers, businessmen, nurses, doctors, and teachers from each country shared ideas and experiences with each other. We not only came to like each other, but, miracle of miracles, we began to love one another. Our fellowship together created lasting friendships grounded in mutual respect and love.

Christian services were conducted in churches, the Nagasaki Cultural Center, many schools, and at the Peace Park located at "ground zero" — the exact spot over which the atomic bomb had exploded thirty years earlier.

The consistent theme of my messages, then, just as it is today, was that the unconditional love of Christ is the most powerful force in the world. More powerful than atomic bombs, Christian love can change hearts, lives, attitudes and actions. We declared that through the death and resurrection of Christ, everyone can experience personal forgiveness and, by God's amazing grace, can love and forgive one another.

Mario Matsufuji had been the Pastor of the Baptist Church in Nagasaki for fifteen years, the same number of years I had pastored at Trinity. Exactly the same age, we had both served in the military of our respective countries, having been trained to fight and kill one another. During the war years, we both had a spiritual experience that led each of us to make a personal commitment to Jesus Christ. Both of us were called by God into the ministry. Understandably, the first time we met in Nagasaki, an instant, profound, and lasting Christian love blossomed between us. God creates phenomenal serendipitous events!

The climax of our Nagasaki crusade, televised throughout Japan, was one of the most exhilarating moments of my life. On August 9, 1975, hundreds attended a service at Peace Park located at "ground-zero." The service coincided with the exact moment the Bomb exploded.

Pastor Matsufuji and I, standing side by side, made exactly the same statement — he in Japanese, and I in English. We said that had we met one another thirty-one years previously, we would have tried to kill each other. In 1975, because of the transforming power of God's love and forgiveness in our lives, our relationship had moved beyond forgiveness and acceptance. We had become brothers in Christ!

All of the experiences in Nagasaki were phenomenal. Our meetings made front-page news every day and national television throughout Japan on a regular basis. The mayor, his wife and the city leaders responded to our overtures of love and fellowship. The mayor's wife, along with the wives of the political and social leaders of Nagasaki, gave a High Tea at the Buddhist Temple honoring Martha. The last honoree for whom this was done in Nagasaki was Queen Elizabeth.

The Japanese made a film of the ten-day event that was shown throughout Japan. An American film crew produced a documentary entitled, "Nagasaki — One Man's Return," that was shown on NBC nationwide in 1976. The film received the Gold Medal at the New York Television and Film Festival as the finest religious program produced in 1976.

Following our visit to Japan, twenty-five Japanese from Nagasaki, including Pastor Matsufuji and Mayor Morotani, accepted our invitation to visit San Antonio where they were warmly greeted by religious, business and political leaders. Mayor Morotani and I, interviewed on the "Today Show" by Edwin Neuman, shared the story of the Nagasaki experience with millions of viewers.

The Nagasaki experience is irrefutable proof that only God can produce transforming change in the human heart. Law never changes the human heart; legislation cannot change the human heart; religion fails to alter the human heart; force never changes hearts. We are absurdly naive if we think we can change hearts by dropping bombs on people who believe differently from us. Man's influence may alter external behavior for a brief time, but only God's love can transform our desires and attitudes forever. After fifty years in the ministry, I know that the living, loving Christ is the only power capable of producing lasting change in a person's life.

When Christ's love is accepted in every heart, all our attitudes and actions will change. We no longer will drop bombs on one another. We will avoid inflicting "verbal bombs" that can cut and hurt one another in our homes, our offices, our communities and our churches.

God's exploding love creates a spiritual "fall-out" of grace and forgiveness that can bring peace to our world. Because of the cross of Christ, the "ground zero" of a new kind of explosion, the explosion of love and forgiveness in the hearts of all mankind, will inactivate all man-made, destructive bombs around the world.

My Japanese experiences introduced me to many masquerading angels who occupy a permanent place in my life. During the autumn of 1945, in a tiny Nagasaki Methodist church, I met some angels masquerading as human bodies scarred by the atomic bomb. Those people whom I had hated at a distance, I began to love when I drew close to them. In nearness or at a distance, Christ makes all of us "one" in love.

Thirty years later, more masquerading angels proved the power of God's transforming love. God can transform those who accept and give His love. Rejoice!

EVERY DOG
HAS HIS DAY

I n the early fifties, I conducted revival crusades sponsored by a local church, or, in many instances, by a combination of churches. These crusades were held in local churches, football stadiums, tabernacles, race tracks — just about anywhere and everywhere. In the South, the most popular meeting place was a circus-like tent.

In a revival sponsored by churches in Lake Charles, Louisiana, the tent, located on a vacant lot across the street from McNeese State College, seated 1,700 people including a choir of two hundred. The planning, praying and preparation for this particular revival had been ineffective, resulting in a dull, stale, flat and unexciting crusade with a congregational attendance no larger than the two hundred member choir.

The unfilled, cavernous tent encouraged all of us to do more to improve attendance and enthusiasm. We prayed. We publicized. We invited people in civic clubs and churches to attend and bring their friends. Despite our best efforts, only a few hundred people attended each night. The revival needed resuscitation. I've been to funerals that had more life than that revival meeting.

My good friend, and co-worker for many years, Eddie Nicholson, was leading the music. Multitalented Eddie, one of the finest congregational song leaders I ever knew, had a beautiful voice, composed extraordinary music, and inspired the best from every choir he led.

Eddie had one shortcoming, however. He thought he could still play the B-flat trumpet as well as he played it in the junior high school band in Cleveland, Tennessee. Eddie was no Gabriel. The walls of Jericho would still be standing if Eddie had been Joshua's trumpeter. I fervently believe that God will select someone other than Eddie to sound the apocalyptic trumpet, because Eddie's discordant notes would cause most of us to miss the resurrection.

I had fun kidding Eddie about his trumpet playing (or his lack, thereof). Eddie, in turn, teased me about things which God has forbidden me to tell (because they are untrue...and I cannot tell a lie). As you can imagine, our sense of fun enabled us to better cope with the day-to-day work pressures and revival disappointments.

(A sense of humor, more than a luxury, is a necessity for everyone, particularly Christians. A joyless Christian is an oxymoron — a contradiction to Christian beliefs. I agree with my good friend and magnanimous Christian, the late Grady Nutt, who said, "Laughter is God's hand on the shoulder of a troubled world.")

Despite my teases about his trumpet playing — or, perhaps, because of them — Eddie would, from time to time, drag out that old B-flat trumpet and try to play. The expectation of singing the revival favorite, *Love Lifted Me,* always foretold trumpet time. This hymn, one of the few that would allow Eddie to hit most of the notes, also gave Eddie a chance to play without being heard. A huge congregation singing one of their favorite tunes, backed by an exuberant choir, and a reverberating organ and piano, allowed many of Eddie's sour notes to fall on deafened ears.

Early in the week of the Lake Charles revival, Eddie whipped out his trumpet and started playing as the small congregation sang, *Love Lifted Me.* Every note that Eddie sounded that night easily penetrated the confines of the sparsely occupied tent. The shrill, discordant notes were enough to make young women cover their ears, babies cry and dogs howl.

On this epochal night, during the second chorus of *Love Lifted Me,* an English bulldog from a nearby neighborhood came tearing down the center isle of the tent, heading toward the speaker's platform where Eddie was playing. Everybody in the choir saw the bulldog coming. Most of the congregation also caught a glimpse of the speeding animal flashing down the sawdust trail toward the front. Soon all eyes were fixed on the dog.

When he reached the base of the front platform, the bulldog spun around in a circle three or four times, howling in agony. But Eddie played on! A caterwauling bulldog spinning in full view of everyone didn't stop Eddie's *Love Lifted Me.*

Suddenly the dog turned and ran, at full speed, down the center aisle toward the exit. Abruptly, the animal stopped, and, as dogs are known to do, cocked a hind leg to relieve himself on the center tent pole. The dog stood there a moment, vigorously kicking up sawdust with his back feet. Then, as proud as any dog who's accomplished nature's task, he strutted calmly out of the tent. The place exploded with laughter! The choir screamed with delight!

Eddie, stunned, gawked at the tent pole, a bewildered look on his face. Suddenly, he turned toward me, pleading, "What did I do?"

Between my convulsions of laughter, I replied, before doubling over, "Eddie, did you see what that dog thought of your trumpet playing!?!?!"

Eddie looked forlornly at his trumpet, which only caused more convulsive laughter.

We tried to recover the service, but every two or three minutes, waves of giggling would spread across the congregation until the entire tent filled with laughter. Finally, I said, unable to control my own laughter, "Folks, I think it's time to go home. I hope you'll come back tomorrow night and bring someone with you, but please leave your dogs at home."

The next day in Lake Charles, the "dog" was the topic of conversation. That night the revival leaders were astounded! Every seat was filled and people were sitting on the ground outside the tent. Although I didn't say anything, I couldn't help but wonder whether the people had come for the revival or to see if the dog would perform again. I had a feeling that the dog had brought the masses, but, whatever the motive, I rejoiced that our tent was overflowing.

The overflow crowd continued throughout the week, allowing a lackluster, turned radiant, crusade to recruit many hearts for Christ. At the conclusion of the revival, we thanked God for all — and I do mean ALL — of our blessings, including the English bulldog's response to Eddie's trumpet, without whose reaction many souls would have remained lost.

God's grace abounded when an English bulldog became inspired by the clashing sounds of Eddie's trumpet. Those who participated in the revival were once again reminded that God can use the most unlikely events imaginable to bless His people.

Later, I told Eddie we should have purchased that dog for our evangelistic work. Anytime a revival failed to meet expectations in numbers or enthusiasm, Eddie could pull out that old trumpet, play *Love Lifted Me,* and we'd turn the dog loose. Eddie took a long while before he laughed.

As important as humor is in helping us live life to the fullest, God's amazing ability to use events to reveal His profound love for us is more valuable. God can take anything — ANYTHING — to produce ultimate good, bringing help to us and glory to Himself. Some of the silliest and dumbest things we have done can be transformed into a message of his unconditional love for us.

The English bulldog revealed God's humanity by showing us His refreshing sense of humor. Our God — a joyful, loving, laughing Heavenly Father — responds to us in a "real" way, a way that allows us to marvel at His understanding of our condition. God is real. He loves us in a "real" way, a way that we can understand.

We like people who are "real," who eschew artificiality and phoniness. Having nothing to hide, they are transparent — "down to earth."

"Down to earth" reminds me of God. A "down to earth" person was born in a manger. He grew up in a carpenter's shop and walked, talked, ate, and celebrated with everyday people, before dying as a common criminal on a Roman cross. On that cross, He took the worst the evil world could accomplish — the dirtiest, filthiest part of our existence — and transformed decay into everlasting life. God turned odious death into the most glorious event the world has ever known — The Resurrection!

By the power of His unconditional love, God transforms our sour notes, our bulldog antics and our foolish mistakes into the laughter of life!

God used a burning bush in the desert to turn old Moses into a fiery servant of God. He used a little rock in the hand of a shepherd boy named David to change the course of world history. He used a donkey to speak to the disobedient prophet, Balaam. He used the lunch of a little boy in Galilee to feed thousands! He took a cruel Roman cross and used it to create a new world! He used an English bulldog to add life to a revival. He created us to glorify Him and enjoy Him forever.

HAILING AN ANGEL

T he year marked the first of over fifteen trips I took to Eastern Europe during some of the worst days of communist domination in that area of the world. A Christian businessman and I wanted to meet Christian leaders in those countries to learn the extent of their suppression so we could formulate a way to bring hope to thousands of forgotten Christians suffering under the tyranny of an atheistic country. On this initial trip, my friend and I visited every country in Eastern Europe, with the exception of Bulgaria and Albania, where we were denied visas.

My businessman friend who graciously provided the trip for me, was instrumental in God's stimulation of my spirit to lead Trinity Baptist Church to begin a ministry of encouragement to Eastern European countries. My friend was the creative force — a masquerading angel — behind our spreading the hope of Christianity to the Communist Eastern block nations.

He and I had been invited by Dr. Michael Zidcoff, pastor of the Moscow Baptist Church, to attend a special May Day worship service in his church. Eager with anticipation, we left our hotel to flag a taxi to take us to church, but, to our surprise and consternation, no taxis were waiting at the hotel cab line where, previously, we had seen dozens of taxis each morning. We walked to the other hotels in the vicinity. Still, no taxis could be found.

In desperation, we hurried to the Entourist Office, the official travel agent of the Soviet Union, to receive assistance. The officials there curtly told us no cabs were available, because May Day, a national holiday, precluded their commercial use.

We, to use the Southern vernacular, were in a fix. With no other alternative, we began walking, hoping we could flag down a disoriented cab driver who had forgotten the day was May first. (That, just as in America, would have been a miracle — no one forgets holidays!) We began waving at every car that even slightly resembled a taxi, but no one responded.

I felt helpless. I prayed, "Lord, we feel you led us to Moscow because you wanted us to be in the church so we could meet and worship with our Russian Christian brothers and bring words of greeting from Christians in America. Lord, I don't believe You led us these thousands of miles to be aimlessly walking up and down the sidewalk looking for a taxi. Please help us."

My friend remained in the street persistently attempting to flag a non-existent taxi as I walked toward the hotel where I saw three men talking with each other. As I strolled by, trying to decide how to initiate a conversation, one man, in broken English, asked if I needed help. I told him how desperate we were to find a taxi to transport us to the Baptist church.

Quickly communicating our predicament to his Russian friends, he asked if I had the address of the church. Sharing the address with him, I inquired if it were possible to walk or take a tram to the church. He explained that the trams, like the taxis, were not operating on May Day and that the church would be impossible to find without a guide.

After the three men talked together briefly, one of the Russians motioned for us to get in his car as the English speaking Russian declared, "He will take you to the church."

Profusely thanking the men, I called to my friend, "I've got a taxi!"

We jumped in the back seat, beginning an adventure that would take us miles through the streets of Moscow. Every now and then our new-made friend would glance back, smiling broadly. After awhile I realized there was no meter in the car. Almost simultaneously, my friend and I recognized that we were in a private automobile!

We also had another surprise. Even without having the address, the Russian knew exactly how to get to the church. Five minutes before the worship service began, we arrived at the large sanctuary. Leaping out of the car, we attempted to pay our driver, but he refused our offer, countering our persistence with a friendly "Nyet."

Then, with a huge smile on his face, he made the sign of the cross, then placed his hands together in prayer. Flooded with the love of the Holy Spirit, we realized God had delivered a Christian driver to us. Smiling beatifically, our masquerading angel drove quickly out of sight. I glanced heavenward, whispering a heartfelt "thanks," as we entered the church, warmed by God's love for us. Stepping over the church threshold, I felt God's soft chuckle in reply.

The worship service, made more magnificent by God's transit surprise, led to future visits that offered the privilege for me to preach in that church and to many other exciting, courageous, and enthusiastic churches throughout Eastern Europe.

Over two thousand worshipers crowded into that sanctuary, designed for a little over a thousand people. The three hour worship service — overflowing with awe-inspiring music, earnest prayer, and fervent preaching — flooded us with the inscrutable power of God's universal love. The knowledge of God's compassion for His people of all nations penetrated our souls deeper than the words that our assigned interpreter translated for us.

During the service, hundreds of people submitted slips of paper on which were written their prayer requests. As the pastor read the requests, I realized that the personal concerns in Moscow were identical to those petitions I hear in San Antonio. Our yearnings acknowledge no boundary lines. All of us — from everywhere — seek and search for the Lord. All people desire reassurance that God loves us, hears us, and will guide us and protect us when we pray.

I felt a deep and profound identification with these devoted, courageous Russians. My spirit filled with compassion and gratitude as I understood, once again, that God loves us all. We are all alike. We share the same hopes, concerns, fears and dreams. We are "One" in the family of faith. How wonderful the world will be when we recognize and remember our "Oneness" in Christ — when we enjoy God and glorify Him together.

What an extraordinary gift of God, we received on May Day, 1968, in Moscow! That day, God divinely impressed my spirit that He will hear us anywhere and make provisions for our needs everywhere.

I remain grateful for the angel masquerading as a Moscow taxi driver who took us to that magnificent church filled with gracious Christians personifying God's universal love. The memory — of the driver's smile, the sign of the cross and the praying hands — reminds me that when we feel as alone as a stranger stranded on a deserted street in Moscow, God comes, often masquerading as an angel, to guide and encourage us.

Someday you may be sitting alone in a surgical waiting room; or you may be forced, by financial crisis, to move to a unfamiliar city; or you may find yourself deserted by friends and family. When those days of loneliness and despair come — as they will, from time to time, for us all — let us remember that God hears our prayers at anytime and from anywhere. God can even hear and answer prayers on the streets of Moscow, then the capital of Communism.

He listens and hears everyone, from all nations, at all times. In the darkest prison, amidst the starving and the abandoned, from the tortured and abused, God hears. From sea to shining sea, from the valleys to the mountains, from the free and the captive, God hears. He drives a cab that stops for all who hail Him.

THE POWER OF ONE

Almost every day for thirty years, I have thought of a woman I met three decades ago. She exemplifies the power of one person to make a difference in the lives of thousands. Whenever I read of wars, destruction, poverty, mayhem, tragedy, man's inhumanity to man — I think of her. The memory of her heroic deed encourages me.

On a beautiful spring Sunday morning in 1969, I was speaking in the Warsaw Baptist Church. Their gifted pastor, Reverend Pawlik, who spoke fluent English, hosted my visit and interpreted my message to his congregation that day.

During the service, Reverend Pawlik acknowledged the return of Mrs. Kamila Michowski, who had been gravely ill for a long while. Her first Sunday back in church coincided with her ninetieth birthday. The congregation, delighted to have Mrs. Michowski worshipping in her usual second row seat, greeted this beloved woman by singing a robust Polish rendition of Happy Birthday. Later, Reverend Pawlik shared Mrs. Michowski's remarkable story with me.

On September 28, 1939, Warsaw fell to Hitler's storming Nazi army. Conquest was only the beginning of the city's anguish. During the Nazi occupation of Poland, Jews, many of whom were deported from regions throughout Western Europe, found themselves penned behind the walls of the Warsaw ghetto. Approximately 40,000 people lived in that area prior to the Nazi offensive. Hitler's demonic plan forced a half-million Jews behind the walls where they vegetated under dreadful conditions, tormented by hunger and disease. Fifty thousand Jews died within the first month.

Mass deportations to the death camp in Treblinka were inaugurated during the summer of 1942 as part of Hitler's "Extraordinary Pacification Action" — the Nazi euphemism for mass murder. The Warsaw ghetto was ultimately obliterated and all of the Jews were either methodically executed or deported.

Hitler's Schutzstaffel, or protection squad, better known — and dreaded — by the initials SS, had been commanded to shoot any Pole considered to be rebellious or politically undesirable. Anyone discovered carrying an item that could be interpreted as a weapon or concealing any sort of anti-Nazi paraphernalia was executed without a trial — often on the spot. Occasionally SS men would leap from a staff car to snatch a suspect. Abrupt arrests by such roaming squads became a prevalent and horrifying event.

During those horrible days of Nazi occupation, Mrs. Michowski, a Christian, would identify herself as a Jew by placing a star of David armband around her bulky coat. Can you imagine? — a Christian disguising herself as a Jew at a time when any slight provocation could cause a dissident to be summarily shot or deported to a place worse than death!

Under her bulky clothing, Mrs. Michowski hid loaves of bread and numerous Bibles; then, armband in place, she would march past the Nazi guarded entrance into the Jewish ghetto. Mrs. Michowski jeopardized her life to take bread and Bibles to those who were physically and spiritually starving. After she had delivered the Bibles, her Jewish friends smuggled her out of the ghetto into the underground sewers from where she made her way back home. On and on she went, week after week, identifying herself publicly as a Jew so she could bring spiritual and physical food to her Jewish neighbors and friends.

Her influence was so profound that the Rabbis would send for Mrs. Michowski when a Jew was near death because the Rabbis believed that their people died more peacefully after they talked to Mrs. Michowski. Hundreds of people received bread and Bibles from this fantastic Christian woman, who so loved her neighbors as herself that she jeopardized her life for their welfare. If there were ever an angel camouflaged as a human being, it was Mrs. Kamila Michowski.

There's a postscript: After the war, the indomitable Polish people, using maps, pictures and drawings, reconstructed the old city of Warsaw in such a dramatic and factual way that it seemed as if the city had never been touched. The Polish people responded to Hitler's hate by rebuilding their city. Today, Warsaw stands as a testimony to the unyielding will of the Polish people. Hitler conquered their city; the spirits of the Polish people remained steadfast.

The Baptist church, too, was reconstructed on the edge of the Warsaw ghetto where it once stood. As construction workers were digging the foundation for the new church, they discovered bones of Jews who had been killed or starved by the Nazi invaders. At the dedication of the church the pastor stood on the reconstructed steps, and with bones in hand, declared, "Our church has been built on the bones of martyrs."

We have martyrs today. Sadly, unlike Mrs. Michowski, we turn our heads and walk the other way, ignoring the thousands of people hungering for both physical and spiritual food.

Mrs. Michowski, who never took just Bibles nor just bread, but always, bread and Bibles, personifies what the ministry and work of the church must be in today's world. With 10,000 people, most of them children, dying each day of hunger (think of the tragedy — 10,000 people starving to death each and every day), churches must be willing to supply both physical and spiritual bread to those in need. We can no longer sit smugly in our pews. We must put on our arm bands and, with bread and Bibles in hand, confront danger by ministering to those in need. The example of Mrs. Michowski and the bones of the martyrs demand action.

Jesus gave both physical and spiritual bread to the multitudes in His day, and He expects us to be carrying out the same dual ministry in our day *(Matthew 9:36-37)*:

> *When he saw the crowds, he had compassion for them*
> *because they were harassed and helpless,*
> *like sheep without a shepherd.*
> *Then he said to his disciples,*
> *"The harvest is plentiful, but the laborers are few.*
> *Ask the Lord of the harvest, therefore, to send out laborers*
> *into his harvest field."*

Ignoring the Bible's command and the example of Jesus, pastors and members of our country's urban churches continue to cover their eyes, failing to see the poverty and hunger all around them, neglecting the needs of the physically and spiritually hungry of our great cities.

The Bible contains four hundred passages on the poor. Sixty-four passages tell believers to help vulnerable people such as immigrants, migrants, widows and the jobless. To fail to meet the needs of these suffering people with bread and Bibles is to disobey our Lord.

Roman Bakke, former pastor of churches in Seattle and Chicago, who currently dedicates a full time ministry to solving inner city challenges, declares, "Many suburban white churches are 'comfort zones' where pastors feed their congregations a 'pabulum diet' when it comes to the needs of those outside their social circles."

He is appalled that "Scripture is ignored" when it comes to the needy. While Christians can't mend everything that's wrong with society, each of us can offer our individual time and talents to help our inner city brothers. Instead of waiting in pious indifference for the return of the Lord, let each of us assume the power we have to make a positive difference in this spiritually and physically starving world.

Our usual response to tragedy involves denial. To a certain extent, denial is a natural protective device. In today's world, we see, hear, and read of tragedy as it unfolds. Television, radio, and the Internet bombard us with atrocities minute-by-minute. The problems of the world seem so vast we feel helpless to do anything. To protect our psyche, we become apathetic to tragedy. Because we feel powerless, we ignore the problems and do nothing.

Here is a suggestion: Whenever you read of atrocities or hear of mistreatments or see examples of man's inhumanity to man, think of Mrs. Michowski. Remembering her will remind you that you can make a difference. You can contribute positively to your circle of influence.

What can you do to reduce suffering in the world? Pray for those in distress? Yes. Encourage those whose profession involves assisting others — preachers, teachers, counselors, police, firemen, social workers? Yes.

How else can you make a difference? Think about your unique gifts. Ask God to help direct your steps toward those you can help. There is a special plan for you. There is something unique for you to do. Be grateful that God — with the indwelling Holy Spirit and with Christ who always walks with you — has given you the power to make a positive difference.

Remember who wins the battle between good and evil. Jesus

wins!!! No matter how hopeless things may appear; no matter how unjust the world seems; no matter how violent, destructive, chaotic, desperate, noisome, frantic, or grave the world appears — remember that nothing can change the ultimate outcome of Christ's victory. Reading Paul's powerful words in *Romans 8:38-39* can sustain us during the world's most troubling times:

> *For I am convinced that neither death nor life,*
> *neither angels nor demons,*
> *neither the present nor the future,*
> *nor any powers,*
> *neither height nor depth,*
> *nor anything else in all creation,*
> *will be able to separate us from the love of God*
> *that is in Christ Jesus our Lord.*

Because Christ sustains us, we can make a difference in our personal world, in our daily encounters, and in our hourly circumstances. The good we do — the bread we give — aids others who, in turn, assist others. Good from our personal world ripples to other personal worlds that, in turn, ripples to other personal worlds. We can — each of us — make a difference.

My life has been blessed by the experience of meeting and talking with Mrs. Michowski, an angel of God camouflaged as a Baptist woman, wearing a star of David, carrying bread and Bibles beneath her clothing, walking boldly past Nazi guards into the horrifying ghetto, and returning to her home through the sewers of Warsaw. She reminds me of the power of one. That power becomes atomic when ignited by the light and love of Christ, the Father, and the Holy Spirit.

Remember Mrs. Michowski — and the power of one. You can make a difference!

AN ANGEL'S NOD

In the summer of 1970, the "Sound Foundation," our remarkable youth choir led by Leroy Yarbrough, then our Minister of Music, toured some of the larger cites in Communist Russia and Eastern Europe. Martha and I, along with our family and a number of adult sponsors, accompanied the choir to Moscow, Leningrad, Warsaw, Prague, Budapest, and Berlin. Having previously been to the Soviet Union, I knew that music, performed in planned church concerts as well as spontaneously in the streets, hotel lobbies, air terminals, bus stops, and restaurants, provided one of the best ways to communicate the gospel.

Previous Russian travels had also exposed me to the country's enormous need for Bibles. Informed by officials that each tourist could bring one Russian Bible into the Soviet Union, we packed our bags accordingly. I had a contact in Moscow to whom I was to deliver the Bibles. He, in turn, would then cautiously distribute them to the people.

At that time Bibles, when available, cost about one hundred rubles on the black market which was the equivalent of one hundred U.S. dollars. Knowing that the Russians were willing to spend that much money from their meager resources to own a Bible, inspired me to do all I could for them. I did not feel we were "smuggling" the Bibles for we intended to give them away, not sell them.

Because no one informed me about the questioning Russian officials in the Moscow airport, we did not try to hide or disguise the Bibles. Each of us had one in our suitcase and felt confident we would be allowed to bring the Bibles into Russia.

After landing at the Moscow airport, about half of our group had cleared customs with their Bibles. Suddenly, the chief customs agent discovered a Bible! Everything stopped! She ordered everyone off the bus and into the airport to be more thoroughly searched. The agents combed through our luggage removing all the Russian Bibles as well as confiscating our own personal English Bibles. They also took our books, magazines, newspapers, cameras, tape recorders, tapes, records, and miscellaneous written material.

After taking the thirty-nine Russian Bibles, they took me! Two soldiers escorted me into a tiny, stark, windowless room where I was questioned for over four hours by as many as four officials at a time. They were very unhappy with me!

These intimidating officials wanted to know everything. They asked where I purchased the Bibles, to whom I planned to sell them, and the amount of profit I expected from the sale.

I told the threatening officials that we were planning to give the Bibles to those who wanted them. They wanted to know if I had an accomplice in Russia.

I refused to identify my confederate, for I knew exposure could cause serious repercussions. I told the inquisitors that we simply desired to give Bibles to any of the people in Russia who wanted them. "We will accept no money for them," I said.

No one believed me. The interrogators commanded that I write about my life and my plans. They wanted a thorough accounting of my genealogy, birth, childhood, education, military experience, occupation, social experiences, and family life. They insisted that I enumerate our plans for our Russian trip. They wanted details on who we planned to visit. They wanted information about our entire group.

I wrote five or six pages. After the inquisitors had returned from reading and discussing my composition, they asked more detailed questions. Soon they knew more about me than Martha. They had me believing I would never see her or my family and friends again.

I have a difficult time explaining how I felt during the four hours of interrogation. Like a six-year-old sent to the principals office for giggling in class? No. Worse than that. Like a junior high quarterback pursed by Mean Joe Greene? Worse. Like a revolutionary confronted by a hooded executioner? Perhaps. None of these descriptions, however, can describe the fear, loneliness, and intimidation I experienced. This was serious business. I felt powerless to help myself. For the first time in my life, I began to fully comprehend what the apostles endured from their persecutors.

Separation from others may be the most fearsome aspect of an interrogation. If the inquisitors were treating me harshly, what might they be doing to Martha and the rest of the group? As each hour slowly passed, I felt more and more concerned about my loved ones and friends.

Finally — and reluctantly — the inquisitors accepted my explanation. Our group, freed from a "smuggling" charge, were permitted to enter the Soviet Union. For the first time in four hours, I saw Martha. Our relief was indescribable, but despite holding each other again, we both remained frightened, intimidated, and discouraged.

Before our release, the chief customs officer confronted us once more. The massive, hostile woman towered over us, her stern countenance revealing her venomous attitude toward our group. As the fierce woman proclaimed her disgust for us in fluent English, Martha, confident and forthright, respectfully questioned her.

"Why does it upset you so much for us to bring Bibles?" she asked.

Having just been through four terrifying hours, I was stunned as Martha continued: "You don't believe the Bible. If you think it contains a collection of fairy tales, why are you threatened by it?"

I stared wide-eyed with gaping mouth as Martha continued to challenge our adversary. For a fleeting moment, I saw myself shoveling Siberian snow as Martha was paraded through the streets of Moscow tied to an ox-cart wearing a sign that read, "Bible Smuggler."

My horrified eyes pleaded with Martha as my mind flooded with thoughts of impending doom. My body language signaled to Martha, "Cool it or we'll be cooling it in Siberia."

To my relief, the custom agent ignored Martha's questions with a smirk.

Martha's undaunting courage emboldened me to ask the agent, "What will happen to the Bibles?"

She curtly answered: "The Bibles will be burned! Every one of them! They will be burned!"

Summoning more courage, I half-questioned, half-stated: "You mean with the price of Bibles one hundred rubles each, you intend to burn them?!"

Unflinching she sternly replied, "The Bibles will be burned."

This woman was as serious as a Salem puritan at a witch dunking.

At that moment, I happened to glance at the thirty-nine Bibles stacked neatly on the custom chief's desk, guarded by an equally serious Russian soldier. To my amazement he had opened one of the Bibles and was reading it.

I instantaneously locked eyes with the guard when the custom chief repeated that the Bibles would be burned. Often a glance says more than a thousand words. The guard's gaze reflected an understanding that surpassed cultural barriers. In this ephemeral moment our spirits met.

Ever so slightly, in a furtive way that no one else would notice, he slowly shook his head back and forth, a delicate, but enchanting smile on his face. His eyes, his head, his smile, his body language all said: "No. These Bibles will not be burned. They will be read!"

As certain as the promise that our Lord will return, as sure as the Bible is God's divine word, I am confident that those Bibles escaped the custom chief's fire, and those thirty-nine holy books have inspired and encouraged hundreds of Russian souls. I am equally certain that the guard was an "angel" masquerading as a Russian soldier.

When I feel trapped and helplessly inadequate, I recall the Russian guard whose silence tacitly indicated a power greater than a roomful of contentious custom chiefs. We can rejoice in the endless supply of "angels" masquerading as human beings who show up in unpleasant places and untenable times. May we all be mindful of God's special emissaries — the angels He provides for us.

By the way, there awaited no Siberian snow shovel for me, and Martha never paraded through Moscow in an ox-cart. Our trip that began with a bust, ended with a bang. God's enduring love gave us reason for continued rejoicing throughout our tour as you will read in the next chapter.

FROM RUSSIA, WITH LOVE: A POSTSCRIPT

As our group boarded a bus and drove away from the Moscow airport, we all experienced an exhilarating sense of relief counterbalanced by an imprisoning dread. I sat with Martha in the seat directly behind the driver. We held hands. The bus was filled with a deathly silence. A mixture of emotions — denial, anger, despair, fear, vindictiveness — tumbled through my heart and mind.

The events of the last four hours seemed to fog over momentarily: *What happened? Was I really mistreated. Yes. I was. They have no right to treat me and my group that way. I'm going to report this incident to the American Embassy. Maybe God will zap my inquisitors with a lightening bolt. Wait a minute. I'm a Christian. I'm supposed to love my enemies.*

I glanced furtively at our Russian guide, Ella, sitting across the aisle from us. Her face was as rigid as carved granite. Was she a guide or a spy? Would she be reporting to the customs chief? Would she prevent us from performing in streets and shopping areas?

As often happens in time of stress, humor came to the rescue. Someone near the back of the bus called out, "Hey, Buckner. Your skin is so green, the Russians ought to send you to Siberia just to bring some color to the place."

Everybody laughed, and we all began to lighten up. I kidded Martha about my vision of her in an ox-cart wearing the sign, "Bible Smuggler" and she chuckled about my bug-eyed look when she questioned the customs chief.

I was bombarded with questions: "What did they say to you? Why were you in there so long? Did they threaten you? Did you ask if you could call your attorney?"

I wanted to know what happened to the others when I was being interrogated. What were they feeling and thinking? Had they considered booking the next flight back to New York?

As the banter became more lively, I again happened to glance in Ella's direction. She remained granite-faced. Throughout the first few days of the trip she persisted — stoic, unreadable.

Then, incrementally, a changed countenance began to emerge. On the long train trip from Moscow to Leningrad, she wanted to know how to play Bridge. As our kids cheerfully taught her, we saw her icy demeanor begin to melt under the warm, loving sun (and Son) of happy Christian teenagers.

Because Russian regulations required scrutiny our movements, Ella attended all our services and concerts. She was present wherever our choir performed or whenever we shared the Christian message. She watched as dozens of Russians renewed their faith or came to Christ for the first time. As this atheist Russian guide attended all of our church services, repeatedly hearing the message of Jesus' love and grace in word and song, her heart softened.

Our last night in Russia, a shock awaited me. We were in a Moscow hotel preparing to leave the next morning when one of the finest young men in our group, Toby Snowden, came to me deeply distressed. Toby, a Baptist minister today, reminded me of a Norman Rockwell poster child. A scholar, athlete, and devoted Christian who, in 1970, was elected Outstanding Teenager of Texas, he epitomized the finest and best in American young people.

Unfortunately, the Russian trip revealed one flaw in Toby's character — absent-mindedness. When unpacking his bags the first night in Russia, he had discovered a Russian Bible that customs had overlooked. The lateness of the hour and the trauma I had endured at the airport discouraged him from disturbing me that night. He tucked the Bible away, vowing to tell me of his discovery the next morning. The excitement of the following morning and the ensuing days made Toby forget his vow. Only when he was arranging his belongings for the trip home did Toby rediscover the Bible. He immediately paled, tucked the Bible under his coat, and rushed to my room.

I must have turned the color of a prospective Siberian evergreen again, because Toby's look reflected pity and remorse — as if he were to blame for my last step to the gallows. Attempting to look brave — but feeling more like Don Knotts than John Wayne — I quickly stuck the Bible in my pocket and whispered melodramatically, "Toby, do not mention this to anyone."

What was I to do? I knew for certain, I was not returning to the Moscow airport with another Russian Bible in my possession! I quickly bid Toby good night and decided to sleep on it — literally. Let me assure you that one fails to sleep well with a Russian Bible tucked under his pillow and visions of monstrous custom agents dancing in his head.

The following morning, I grabbed a copy of *Pravda,* the Russian newspaper, and concealed the Bible in the paper. As the bus was loading for our trip to the airport — not knowing what else to do and figuring this was a better approach than facing customs again — I, with great trepidation, took Ella aside privately and said: "Ella, we've made a mistake. It was unintentional, but we have just discovered one Bible that was overlooked at the airport."

She stared back at me, unblinking, while I continued: "I have the Bible wrapped in this newspaper and I'm either going to walk over there and throw it in that trash can or I'm going to give it to you, but I'm not leaving this hotel with it. What shall I do?"

I saw genuine hope beaming from Ella's eyes as she searched all around us, making certain that no one could overhear our conversation: "May I have it? I want to know more."

A radiant peace seemed to surround us as I handed her the Bible camouflaged in the Communist newspaper.

Our trek through customs proceeded uneventfully, almost agreeably. We were pleasantly surprised when the inspectors returned some of the personal items — tape recorders, tapes, and records — they had seized earlier. They failed, however, to return any Christian literature or our English Bibles.

With the newspaper held tightly under her arm, Ella accompanied us to the plane. Our hearts were warmed as she nodded farewell to each of us as we made our way up the airplane's ramp. How different she was — her eyes temperate, her face serene — as she clutched the newspaper-hidden Russian Bible under her left arm and waved fondly to us with her right hand.

I was the last to enter the plane, and as I turned to look back at Ella, she bowed her head ever so slightly as she mouthed so no one else could see, "Thank you."

I never saw the chief of customs or Ella again. As the years progress, my recollection of the interrogation fades in comparison to the brilliant light of the angel, Ella, head bowed in reverential respect to the Mighty One whose peace is stronger than fear and whose love she was beginning to seek out.

What a thrill and reassurance God gives us when he uses our oversights and mistakes to communicate His Word to unlikely people in unlikely places. The absent-minded outstanding Texas teenager brought the hope of the Bible to an atheist and the good news of Jesus Christ came wrapped in the bad news of *Pravda*.

God can even "camouflage" the Bible in the official daily newspaper of an atheistic government! *Pravda* means "Truth," but it never contained the truth the way it did that day when Ella held it tightly under her arm in the Moscow airport!

With God, all things are possible!

THE STRONG
RIGHT ARM OF GOD

I n the 1980s, I was invited for a two week speaking tour in Yugoslavia, where Communist domination had, for decades, restricted the freedom of worship. A group of our Trinity members traveled with me. The primary purpose of our trip centered on communicating inspiration and encouragement to our Yugoslavian Christian brothers and sisters.

The need for Christian encouragement there overwhelmed us. To better meet the needs of the Yugoslavian people, we organized our group into teams of three to minister to those numerous churches hungering for hope.

While there, as well as in many other communist countries where God privileged me to preach, I recalled George Elliott's famous statement: "What are we here for, if not to make life less difficult for each other?"

We spent several days in the beautiful city of Novi Sad, where we ministered to the students and faculty of the Baptist seminary and preached at a number of churches there. While serving in Novi Sad, we were invited to travel a few miles north to a marvelous city on the Danube, Bakepetrovak, which, in English, means "Peter's Garden."

On Sunday morning, I, along with three others, visited a large country church north of Bakepetrovak, where I was invited to preach the morning message. A seminary professor from Novi Sad, who accompanied us, served as my translator. After the service, we were invited to dinner in the home of one of the most active and devoted members of the church.

Following a delicious meal, we toured his bountiful farm. We spent the rest of the afternoon talking about the pressure on fellow Christians, walking over the farm, and enjoying fellowship with each other.

In that relaxed atmosphere, this gracious gentleman, in an apparently humorous vein, asked me if I would consider coming to serve as pastor of their church. Initially, his smiling eyes made me think he was joking. Suddenly, pausing, he seemed serious. He offered a piece of farm land that would enable me to support myself as I preached the hope of Jesus Christ to the Bakepetrovaks.

I assured the good man that the miracle-working God of Abraham, Isaac, and Jacob — the God of the Red Sea crossing; the God of the manna miracles; the God of the crumbling walls of Jericho; the God of the final grand defeat of the antichrist — had one limitation. He could never turn Buckner Fanning into a farmer. Though the spirit was willing, Buckner's thumb would remain greenless, from the past to forevermore.

He laughed uproariously, shaking the walls of his sturdy little farm home. After what seemed minutes of continuous laughter, the man became serious. He wanted to tell us an indisputable farming miracle.

Upon our initial introduction to the farmer, all of us had noticed that he had no right arm. I silently wondered how he could be a successful farmer with this severe handicap. I, as well as the others in our group, suspected that his son, or, perhaps, his wife performed most of the farm work. In the course of the day, we learned that the farmer's son, endeavoring to get a college education, lived and worked in Belgrade. The farmer's wife suffered from a life-threatening heart condition, restricting her work capacity. To complicate matters, this one-armed farmer, and his seriously ill wife, had the responsibility of caring for his wife's invalid mother. What burdens some of us bear!

With deep feeling, the farmer told us that several years ago, working alone in the fields, his arm had become entangled in some farm machinery. Unable to free himself, he was too far from his house for his cries to be heard. Only after dark, did anyone begin looking for him. By the time he was found, he had lost enough blood to kill most people. Following emergency treatment at a local hospital, he was transferred to a Belgrade medical center where doctors amputated his right arm.

The distance to Belgrade, a day-long train trip from his home, limited visits from his ailing wife. Once each week, she would spend the night at the Belgrade hospital, returning the following day to their home to care for her invalid mother. Christian neighbors worked his farm along with their own. (Obviously, an entire colony of masquerading angels had their membership in the Bakepetrovak church.)

Our trusting friend shared his deepest feelings about those dark days. He became so depressed, he begged God to allow him to die. His thoughts, burdened with hopelessness and helplessness, filled his spirit with despair. He remembered saying to himself: "I have no right arm. No insurance. No help. I'll be a terrible burden to my family and friends. They, who already have more troubles than they can handle, will have a better life without me. God, please let me die."

Late one night, he slipped out of bed, crept to the end of the deserted hall, and tried to raise the hospital's sixth floor window to jump to his death. He couldn't budge the window. He stood at the window, angry and crying, frustrated that his one good arm had insufficient strength to raise the window. In great despair, he returned to his bed, pleading, "God, please let me die."

We sat motionless in that little dining room, as he paused for a long moment. Then, with profound feeling and obvious humility, he interrupted the silence, "God spoke to me in my time of deepest despair. God said, 'Trust Me. Put your faith in Me. I will be your right arm!'"

Many weeks passed before the farmer had sufficiently recovered to return home, where he attempted to resume his farming. He discussed the difficult adjustment period that initially discouraged him. Many times he was tempted to give up, but God's promise kept him going.

Pausing, a huge smile flooding his strong, weathered face, he quietly said, "It may be hard for you to believe, but I want to tell you something — something my wife, my son and my friends can verify. My farm is now functioning more successfully and efficiently than ever before. I am able to accomplish more with one hand than I was ever able to accomplish with two! We're more prosperous today than ever. Life could not be better. God — just as he promised — has been my right arm!"

We may fail to understand why God allows bad things to happen to good people, but we can be certain that "in all things God works for the good of those who love him, who have been called to his purpose" (*Romans 8:28*).

The main question in the book of *Job* has never been more timely than in our age, when the good our country has cultivated for over two centuries seems to have become shredded by evil: Why do bad things happen to good people? Why do Christians suffer troubles? Why does evil, at times, overwhelm good?

Job's counselors assumed that difficulties come to people because they sin. We make the same mistake today, when we claim that sickness or failure results from unconfessed sin or lack of faith.

Tragedy occurs because we live in a fallen world. When we face trials and dilemmas, God desires to show His compassion and love for us. No matter how bad things may seem to be now, we must remember that, in the end, those who love God will be victorious.

> *So do not fear, for I am with you;*
> *do not be dismayed, for I am your God.*
> *I will strengthen you and help you;*
> *I will uphold you with My righteous right hand.*
>
> *Isaiah 41:10*

In those times in my life when I have felt handicapped — cut-off, hurt, afraid, and alone in the darkest moments of the night — I've remembered what God told the Yugoslavian farmer; he told us through Isaiah:

> *I will uphold you with My righteous right hand.*

Through the recollection of the inspirational visit to a one-armed farmer, I have been reminded that in one way or another — through one person or another — God will show up on the scene of our despair to be our salvation, our right arm.

If God can be the right arm of a farmer in Yugoslavia, He can, and will, be your right arm. Whatever your situation may be, He will be with you to hold you. He will lift you. He will bring you through all the "Dark nights of the soul."

When we are weak, or injured, or discouraged, the Lord will take hold of our hand, firmly holding us, guiding us through the exigencies of life.

> *If the Lord delights in a man's way,*

He makes his steps firm;
though he stumble, he will not fall,
for the Lord upholds him with His hand.

Psalm 37:23-24

Remember: God is the one who does the holding! Instead of expecting us to hold His hand (for we are often too weak to hold on), He has promised that He will hold our hand. He will never leave us nor forsake us.

Where can I go from your Spirit?
Where can I flee from Your presence?
If I go up to the heavens, you are there;
if I make my bed in the depths, you are there.
If I rise on the wings of the dawn,
if I settle on the far side of the sea,
even there your hand will guide me,
your right hand will hold me fast.

Psalm 139: 7-10

In God's words, I remember the testimony of a one-armed Yugoslavian farmer, who was for me, and has been for many, one of God's masquerading angels. They are everywhere. We can see them, when we stop plucking the world's blackberries long enough to look.

To which I hear the Yugoslavian farmer adding, "Fantastic! Amen!"

GOD DRIVES
A PICKUP TRUCK

He was in his eighties — tall, gaunt, pale — his hazel eyes daunted, almost hollow. I'd never seen him before. Some members of his family had suggested he make an appointment.

We spent a few minutes in casual talk — what I call, "get acquainted" talk: "Do you know ... ? Have you been to ... ?"

Suddenly, without warning, like a hurting child pleading to a parent, he said, "Buckner, I need help ... help me ... please!"

He looked down, as if embarrassed by his outburst and then gazed out the window at nothing in particular, as though he didn't know how to continue. He seemed to be thinking in slow motion.

From where I was sitting, I could see the setting sun casting orange light on the tall steeple atop our church. This steeple always reminds me to look up to God for help and guidance. As I gazed into the troubled face of this man whose days were growing short, his eyes reflected the despair and hopelessness of a life lived without the comfort of God's redeeming love. His vacant stare and darkened spirit made the room feel cold.

I thought of Lord Byron's lines from "On my Thirty-Sixth Year":

My days are in the yellow leaf;
The flowers and fruits of love are gone;
The worm, the canker, and the grief
Are mine alone!

Suddenly, his countenance changed, as if a mask had been thrown aside revealing an expression of fear — a fierce and desperate terror. I saw him as a man clinging to a cliff, his perilous grip crumbling in his hands, as he anticipated a crash at the bottom of the precipice where darkness would hide him in a lonely death.

"Buckner, I'm dying. They can't stop the cancer. It's devouring me second by second. Surgery, radiation, chemotherapy — nothing can stop the eating away of my life. The best doctors money can buy tell me it won't be long — maybe a few months, more likely a few weeks."

He looked into my eyes, anticipating my next question.

"Pain? Yes, I'm in pain, terrible pain! Thank God for morphine! It eases the physical pain, but drugs do nothing for the deep, aching pain in my heart. That's why I'm tormented. That's what makes dying so agonizing, so frightening."

There was a moment of silence. He seemed to relax a little. A deep fatigue replaced the initial outburst of confession. Breathing a little more slowly, he became philosophical, speaking in low, measured words.

"You know, Buckner, we hear about an aching heart. I've heard you like country-western music, so I know you've heard the song 'My Aching Heart.' We say, 'My heart aches for you.' I thought that was...what do you say...a metaphor? But the heart does ache. Literally. Terribly."

I responded, "Yes, I've heard that song, and I've had some experiences in my own life that made my heart ache."

He paused, seeming to feel that I could empathize with him to a degree, so he continued.

"I lie in bed at night, fitfully. The sedatives don't help much. Occasionally, I doze, but I fight it. I dread going to sleep. I'm afraid I won't wake up."

Without waiting for a reply, he rushed on as if carried by his own words. "Buckner, all I can see is a bottomless pit. My sins overwhelm me — pulling me down, down into the deep darkness of sleep. Then I shudder awake — cold, sweating — only to be pulled once more, deeper and deeper into this gaping pit. My heart is crushed with the pain of my sins."

And then more anguish poured from him like burning lava from an erupting volcano.

"Each night as I lie in my bed, fighting sleep, I confess my sins — over and over and over again — terrified that if I might omit one, it would be the sin that would cause me to spend eternity without God. I confess every sin, repeatedly — every one I can remember. There have been so many. I have used people, damaged people, destroyed others. I've hurt my wife, my family, my associates, myself. My agony comes from the fear that I can't remember all the people I have wounded and all the wrongs I've done. I fear that if I don't confess each one of those sins, I will go to hell. I can't sleep at night because I keep reviewing the events of my past, trying to confess everything."

He related that, as a boy, he had grown up in a church with a strong emphasis on judgment and condemnation that made him feel that if any sin went unconfessed, he would spend eternity without God. He seemed as helpless as a little boy or a wet puppy. I hurt for him, and urgently prayed: "Please, dear Lord, help me know what to say to this troubled man."

I must confess that I also felt a deep anger toward a religion — any religion or any misinterpretation of Christianity — that would create a critical and judgmental atmosphere in which children miss the joy and peace of God's love for all.

He then added, "When I confess my sins, no relief comes. Only fear — fear that there is more sin than I can remember. I'm afraid to sleep, afraid that if I die before confessing everything, I will be lost."

He looked at me like a drowning man crying out for rescue, pulled down with all of his past sins and knowing that he was going down for the third time. He then asked rhetorically: "How could I have gone so wrong?"

As he talked, I felt no anger toward him, just compassion. His story reminded me of the statement, "The chains of habit are too weak to be felt until they are too strong to be broken."

(Forty years of memories rushed through my mind — memories of countless people burdened and frightened about life and death:

...the murderer running from the law in a Midwestern city who came to ask what he should do. After a long discussion I told him to confess his sin to God, return home, and surrender. He served his time and found the peace that God gives to all with a contrite heart.

...a young man dying from AIDS who asked if he could go to heaven. I told him that just as those with cancer or heart disease can go to heaven so could those dying of AIDS. I reminded him that all of us have sinned, though we have not all sinned alike. All who accept Jesus as their Savior can enter God's eternal kingdom because of God's unconditional grace.

...others — so many others — wracked with the guilt of adultery or incestuous behavior. Family members have come questioning suicide by a loved one. I have heard remorse over rape, white collar crime, bankruptcy, drugs, alcohol, family desertion, jealousy, envy, pride. I have endeavored to explain to all who seek my counsel that God forgives the guilt of our sin, and, though the consequences remain, God can rebuild relationships, renew marriages, restore hope and reestablish happy, meaningful lives. Some scars remain, but the wound is healed.

We all have scars. The most respected and revered people in the community have scars. We all sin. I rejoice in sharing the promise of God who said, *Though your sins be as scarlet, they shall be as white as snow; though they be red like crimson, they shall be as white as wool.* This cleansing is for all of us and each of us.)

He continued, "Buckner, I could go on and on giving the depressing details. There is so much to tell, so many sins. I can't remember them all. I've hurt so many people — betrayed and disappointed them. Worst of all, I used God to further my success.

I'd go to church regularly because I felt it did wonders for my reputation. I prayed and would make gifts that were conspicuous and would draw attention to myself. I was doing the right thing, I suppose, for all the wrong reasons. People thought I was really a decent guy, right? I guess the thing that frightens me and hurts me the most is to know I betrayed God so terribly, and I don't think He can forgive me."

He seemed hesitant as he fidgeted with his wristwatch. "I don't know why I came to see you really. Well, yes, I guess I do, I thought maybe by telling you these things I could sleep easier. Shoot straight with me. Can I be forgiven? Is there any hope for me?"

I leaned forward, my arms resting on my knees, my hands were folded, prayer-like.

"Of course, you can be forgiven. God forgives us all. God's grace will save us all. We are not saved by our good deeds, nor are we condemned because of our sinful deeds. The only condemnation is when we reject God's love...God's Grace...God's unconditional forgiveness."

I wanted time to tell him of the prodigal son, the woman caught in the act of adultery — tell him of a God who rejoices over a wandering, lost sheep that He has found. I wanted him to understand what God had done for me and for countless others. Before I could say anything more, he twisted in his chair, and I felt that for a split second there was a flash of change in his eyes. He seemed to be looking at a distant ray of light — possibly a ray of hope for deliverance.

"I'd like to ask you about a dream I had a few days ago. I guess that's one of the main reasons I came. The dream seems so ... well ... Biblical, I guess. I felt strangely comforted — the first comfort I'd experienced in a long, long time, but there was also a frustration about the dream as if I had arrived home, but could not find the key to open the door."

I replied that though I'd had no formal training in dream interpretation, the Bible contained examples — Joseph, Daniel, and others — who could, with God's help, discern the meaning of dreams. I told him that I would be pleased to listen, and, praying for God's help, perhaps we could decipher the dream together.

Without pausing, he began to speak, slowly at first, then expectantly. He prefaced his dream by telling me that he was a lapidarian. He had been fascinated by rocks all of his life.

"I'm a devoted rock hound. I collect them. Cut them. Polish them. Make cufflinks. Jewelry. Just about everything. I love rocks. I've loved them all my life."

He looked at me as if to see if I thought he was a strange creature for having such a hobby. I smiled and congratulated him and indicated that I wanted to hear the rest of the story.

"In my dream, I was standing in this beautiful, green, rolling meadow, as beautiful a field as you've ever seen. A death-like stillness was all around me. I felt as if I were the only person within a thousand miles. It was like one of those early mornings when you are all alone and the ground is covered with dew. A slight, smoky-like fog hovered over the green grass. Then, indistinct images appeared, like vapors escaping from the ground. Mysterious objects began to appear across the meadow. Gradually, I could see them clearly. Rocks. Rocks. Hundreds of rocks. More rocks than I could count, littered the grassy field. Walking closer, I met with a sickening surprise. Moving from rock to rock, I saw, carved on each granite slab, a description of one of my sins. One rock, one sin, with names, dates and horrible deeds."

Without pausing, he continued, more hopeful and excited now.

"I looked across the field, up the grassy knoll and beyond. As far as I could see, the field was covered with protruding rocks and slabs. As I stood contemplating how to remove those rocks, a most surprising event occurred! A pickup truck drove into the middle of the rock-covered field, and a young man, who reminded me of my son, began loading those rocks in the truck.

"I stood transfixed with fascination as he drove off with a full load, only to return again and again, until he had hauled away all of those rocks leaving the green, grassy meadow brilliant with sunshine. The rocks were all gone!

"When I awoke, I had an exhilarating sense of freedom that, sadly, lasted but for a brief moment and again my heart was flooded with fear and dread. Still, there is some comfort when I recall that dream, but I don't understand it."

He stopped and looked at me expectantly. I could tell he had more to say, but he was tired.

Looking over his shoulder, I could see outside the window of my office a beautiful colored tree that was in full bloom. The afternoon sun gave the room a serene, sweet, soothing warmth. I sensed a quivering stillness in the room, like the silent anticipation we experience in the calm before the storm. A strange, indescribable impression filled that room, as if someone had entered, unseen, and, I, like John Wesley, felt my heart strangely warmed. Without question, God was in this moment. Overwhelmed with compassion and peace, I felt a great personal release from anxiety about being able to help the man. God's presence had lifted a heavy burden from my shoulders.

As I looked at the man, I began smiling and suddenly laughed with a joy created by being reminded by this story — full of God's incredible love — of His amazing, creative ingenuity. What a dream-giver He is!

He stared at me a little puzzled because of the big smile on my face. I looked into his questioning face and said, "Sir, God drives a pickup truck!"

"What?"

"Yes, don't you see? God drives a pickup. I want you to think back on that dream. You said that the young man in your dream looked like your son. Is that right?"

"Yes, he sort of reminded me of my son."

"Well, I want you to take a closer look. Rethink that moment, and I'm confident you will see that young man represented more than your son. He was God's son. Jesus Christ drove that truck and carried away all of your sins in a strong bed, double-shock, pickup truck. As the commercial says, it was built 'like a rock.' For God Himself is the Rock of Ages, and He has the strength to carry away and discard forever all of your sin-carved rocks."

A sudden and unexpected inspiration grabbed my mind. "By the way, what did the pickup look like?"

He seemed puzzled. "Well, let's see. It was huge. A big truck, with a wide cab...a narrow bed. Yes, the pickup bed was narrow. I remember in my dream briefly thinking what a large, funny looking pickup."

"Like a cross?"

"Yes, I suppose. Yes. Yes. Yes, it was. The truck — wide cab, narrow bed — was shaped like a cross."

I cannot remember being so fascinated and touched by God's wonderful message coming in such a creative, fresh and personal way to this desperate man searching for hope.

"God is telling you exactly what He promised to do with His son, Jesus Christ. He is personally reminding you what He has told us in His word. He has taken away all your sins and dumped them into the depths of the sea. He says He will remember them against you no more. They're gone! You can forget them because He has! They're gone ... forever ... and ever! Jesus has hauled away all your sins in a pickup shaped like a cross."

He was stunned. Amazed. Slowly, a smile crossed his countenance, and, for the first time, there was a spark of life in his eyes. And then suddenly, his head fell forward into his cupped hands, his elbows resting on his knees. He sobbed uncontrollably.

I let him cry. I knew exactly what was happening in his heart, for it had happened in my heart time and time again in those grace-filled moments that come into our lives unexpectedly and reveal to us the unconditional love of our great God opening the flood gates of cleansing and reconciliation. I knew exactly what he was feeling — joy...gladness... unworthiness...a sense of disbelief that God could love him so...amazement that God's tender love had always been with him...a worshipful feeling of thanksgiving... reverential respect and trust...a burning desire to show God's love to others — all wrapped in the loving arms of the truck-driving Jesus. As we sat there quietly, I refreshed my own experience of the presence of Jesus, while I thanked Him again for His glorious compassion for each and all of us.

The man's sobbing turned to soft crying, a cry of peace and joy. He stood up, put his frail arms around me and kept saying, "Thank you. Thank you."

He talked about feeling flooded with forgiveness. We talked a little more about God's amazing grace. Before he left, we prayed together.

He had gone through the door and suddenly stopped and turned around and came back and asked me if I would conduct his funeral service. "Of course, I will do anything you ask me to do."

I hesitated, wanting to get the words right. "I want to ask you to do something for me...but before you answer, I suggest you think and pray about my request. With your permission, I would like to tell your story — and your dream — at your memorial service, if that would be acceptable to you."

I paused and said, "I won't mention a thing about this without your full agreement."

He could not reply quickly enough. "Buckner, I don't have to think about that request. I don't have to pray about it. Certainly, I want you to tell my story — my entire story. Tell my story at my memorial service, preach about it, mention it on television, write about it, tell it everywhere. Yes, I want you to tell my story — in fact, I beg you to tell my story. I want everyone to know about God's forgiveness, about His compassion, about His love for a degraded sinner like me.

At my service, some of the people I have wronged will be there. I want them to know my remorse and my joy. I want them to know that God forgives me. I want them to know the grace of God will give them great joy and peace. I pray that they will forgive me, too."

As he left the room, he turned, grinning, "I'm not going to have any more problems sleeping...or dying."

A few weeks later, I told his story at the memorial service. I related to the large crowd present the good news that God drives a pickup truck. I told them that God will drive right into the middle of any and every life ... pick up all the junk ... all the garbage ... all the rocks ... all the sins ... load them on the cross-shaped pickup and take them away as far as the East is from the West!

After I concluded the story and pronounced the benediction at the end of the service, no person stirred. It seemed as if everyone had stopped breathing for a moment. There was a powerful sense of reverential awe. Then a remarkable thing began to occur spontaneously. Throughout the congregation, people began to quietly sob. Some hugged one another. People sought each other out. There was a magnificent, divine mixture of crying and laughing in that room. Everyone seemed to be feeling the presence of God's unconditional love and His amazing grace.

In my imagination, I could see God was very busy in that room that day, loading up rocks in his cross-shaped pickup truck. And I could see him driving into the middle of lives and turning the rocky terrain of guilt and sin into a beautiful, green field of forgiveness and peace.

Yes, God really does drive a pickup truck and He really does carry away every one of our sins. Rejoice in that!

He can and will haul your sins away, too. Just let Him drive into the middle of your life, and He will load up your sins and discard them forever.

His truck is warmed and waiting, and Jesus is behind the wheel and ready to come.

He handles all loads.

A BURNING BUSH
ON A RAINY NIGHT

O nce upon a time, long before ATMs, I found myself needing some change. (Yes, Virginia, an era existed when banking hours meant something. Even more unbelievable — a time prevailed before charge cards. This truth, however, may be too offensive to merit discussion in a book intended for a general audience.) Nonetheless, back in the dark ages, when people actually carried money in their wallets, I found myself in an embarrassing situation.

After taking a friend to the airport on a rainy, cold Saturday afternoon I exited short-term parking. When I reached in my pocket to pay the attendant, I realized I didn't have a cent! I was flat broke!

As the rain poured, I told the toll booth attendant my fiscal failings: "Sir, I apologize. I owe you fifty cents, but I don't have a dime. May I leave my watch with you as security, drive home, and return with some money?"

He replied, "There's no need to leave your watch. Just return with the money."

I drove away.

Upon arriving home, Martha informed me of an emergency. A hospital had called to forward an urgent request from a family that I visit their critically ill loved one. I immediately left for the hospital.

My hospital visit lasted more than an hour.

By the time I returned home, the night weather had turned colder. As my unfinished Sunday sermon swirled through my mind, my tension rose with the deepening darkness.

On Saturday nights, most pastors become as restless as a wayward West Texas tumbleweed. Every Sunday is "D-Day" — Delivery Day. With three worship services and other special demands on Sunday, pastors feel a little like General Eisenhower felt the night before "D-Day" in World War II. Saturday night begs for tranquility to allow pastors final preparation and prayer time for Sunday.

As I settled down in my study to polish my thoughts on the next day's sermon, the cold winter wind rattled the driving rain against the window panes. I shivered, shifting in my chair, grateful for the cozy warmth of the room.

Suddenly, I remembered the man in the toll booth. Just as quickly, I began to rationalize: *Remember, Buckner, the four thousand people who will hear you tomorrow in church will want you to be in top form. You have a vital responsibility in the morning. You will be serving God by sharing with people the most important subject in the world. You need to spend some more time in study and prayer. One of the most important things in your life right now is preparing for tomorrow.*

My thinking seemed unflawed. I sounded really good to me.

Oh, what a terrible capacity for self deception all of us humans possess. We have perfected the art of equivocating by using the term, "God's will," to justify personal pursuits. Another frequently misused phrase — "God led me into this decision" — often supports actions that, when closely analyzed, diametrically oppose God's standards.

Considering the Holocaust, the Inquisition, countless "Holy Wars," and the fighting in Ireland, Yugoslavia, and the Middle East, as well as numerous personal ways we deceive ourselves, all of us would do well to pause daily, praying the words from

Psalm 139: 23-24:

> *Search me, O God, and know my heart;*
> *test me and know my anxious thoughts.*
> *See if there is any offensive way in me,*
> *and lead me in the way everlasting.*

At the time, though, *Psalm 139* was being replaced with my brilliant justifications:

Buckner, you don't need to go out in the winter rain to pay that man fifty cents. You might catch a cold that would prevent you from preaching tomorrow. Remember all the times you've been overcharged and didn't get your money back. Refusing to pay this fifty cents will help make things even. Besides, the man has probably forgotten all about it anyway. He's probably already tucked himself warmly into bed.

We can all rationalize our way out of doing what we know is right. God said our hearts are "desperately wicked and deceitful above all things." Deceiving myself that night, I came to the conclusion that our worst lies are the lies we tell ourselves.

While I was justifying my need to stay home, a "still small voice" reminded me of my promise. As the rain continued to pour through the cold night, preparing for Sunday morning became more difficult. When I tried to pray about my sermon, I visualized the man in the toll booth holding out his hand for the fifty cents. Finally, disgusted with my equivocations, I borrowed fifty cents from Martha. Leaving the cozy confines of confabulation, I faced the cold, wet reality of commitment.

Arriving at the airport, I had to dash about thirty rain drenching yards to access the toll booth. Much to my surprise, the man was still there. Shivering from cold, with water dripping from my raincoat,

I, omitting the full details of my rationalizations, said: "Sir, I'm sorry to be so late. I had an emergency visit with a church member in the hospital. I finally made it back with the fifty cents I owe you."

With a smile, he replied, "Reverend Fanning, thank you for coming back. I knew you'd show up because I see you nearly every morning on television. Every time you are on TV, you spend those thirty seconds talking about God and His love. I knew I could trust you."

Shaking hands with my new-made friend, I thanked him for his patience. Running back to my car, I realized I had just seen a "burning bush" that the rain could not extinguish.

God used an unexpected source — a burning bush — to make an impact on Moses. God may use unusual circumstances to communicate with us. When we become open to seeing and hearing God's message from unanticipated situations, we will be surprised with joy — and sometimes with fear. On this occasion, my knees were shaking from reverential respect and awe — from fear. God had just revealed how perilously close I had come to betraying Him.

I sat in the car for a few minutes and, with a trembling and repentant heart, prayed. I thanked God for this "burning bush" which He used to reveal to me that I must always, in every situation, prayerfully endeavor to do what is right rather than what's convenient.

In the presence of this "burning bush," I mentally removed my shoes and praised God:

Dear Lord, thank you for using this experience to trouble my mind and spirit. Please, please never allow me to be undisturbed by your Spirit when I'm about to do something wrong. I nearly betrayed you for fifty cents. Judas did it for thirty silver coins. I was nearly a cheap Judas. Thank you, Lord. Thank you for the "burning bush" in the rain.

AN ANGEL
TO LEAN ON

In 1965, our church began the Alpha Home, a half-way house providing rehabilitation for women suffering from chronic alcohol and substance abuse. Open to any and all women regardless of race or religion, Alpha Home, for many years, provided the only facility for women alcoholics in San Antonio, also reaching to many other parts of this country.

Alpha Home began small, but through the years has grown and expanded. Today hundreds of women who have lived at Alpha Home have come to experience physical, spiritual, and emotional healing. Through a dedicated staff of former alcoholics and numerous volunteers, a loving, nurturing, Christian atmosphere continues to provide strength and encouragement.

Alcoholics Anonymous meetings, group and individual counseling sessions, Vocational Rehabilitation Programs and regular Bible study are all part of the ministry. The Texas Rehabilitation Commission reported our success rate at eighty-six percent, far exceeding the statistical success of secular rehabilitation centers — and for that we are indeed grateful.

One day, the director of our staff, whom I will call Jane, brought a new resident, whom I will call Mary, to my office for a visit. Mary, who had seen me on television, expressed the desire to talk with me personally. I greeted Mary warmly. As the three of us sat together, I told Mary that her decision to seek help pleased me.

I said, "We are very glad you're here and want to you know how eager we are to help you. We will be praying for you. God loves you.

He wants His love to be a powerful force in your life that will help produce spiritual and physical health."

I began to tell Mary that she could lean on God for help. I never finished the sentence. When she heard the phrase — "if you will just lean on God" — she exploded!

Mary's eyes flashed in anger as she harshly said, "Don't tell me to lean on God. I'm not about to lean on God. Every time I've gone near a church or a bunch of Christians they put me down. They made me feel worthless and rejected. I don't want to have anything to do with God or church people. In fact, I don't even believe in God at all!"

I was stunned into silence. Her verbal detonation had rocked me back on my heels. I was speechless. I just sat there.

Jane, seated beside Mary on the couch, gently placed her hand on the hand of the angry young woman. Softly she said, "It's all right. If you don't believe in God, that's all right. I understand. You don't have to lean on God. Why don't you just lean on me and I'll lean on God."

God's love began to grow in Mary's life, much in the way that a seed grows in a vegetable garden. A farmer prepares the soil. A seed is planted. Nothing happens for awhile. At least, nothing is observed. Underneath the earth, miraculous changes occur. The experienced farmer knows that what he fails to see, will certainly appear. He waits patiently for his belief to be made manifest in the miracle of growth. One day a tiny plant appears. The farmer waters and fertilizes the plant. The farmer rids the garden of harmful insects. The plant grows — bountifully. Abundant fruit appears. The wise farmer glorifies God, because without the miracle of growth, no garden produces.

The Spirit of God works the same way. Quietly and deliberately

God changes those who put their faith and trust in Him. No differences are evident at first. Then a tiny modification occurs that blossoms into a new creature, producing the fruit of the spirit — "love, joy, peace, patience, kindness, goodness, faithfulness, gentleness, and self-control" (*Galatians 5:22*).

The Spirit of God works quietly, deliberately — day after day, decade after decade. In the beginning, God brought order out of chaos as His Spirit moved over the deep. Even in times of great dramatic suddenness, as at Pentecost, the moving Spirit of God has been generating beneath the surface of time, preparing for the day when He would burst upon the surface of a fallen world in a fiery, volcanic explosion of creative grace that would perpetually pour out on the world a loving lava-flow of forgiveness and new life!

Following our visit with Mary, nothing seemed to be happening for a long time. But something was happening. One Sunday morning in the worship service, I caught a glimpse of Mary sitting on the back row. She was there again a Sunday or two later. And then again. She began to move a few seats forward in the sanctuary.

Months went by. Then one Sunday morning during the invitation, as I was standing at the front visiting with a family who had come to join our fellowship, I looked to my side. There Mary stood. With tears streaming down her face, she said, "I love Him and I trust Him."

Jane came forward to sit beside Mary, as she had sat beside her on the couch in my office months before. Once again, Jane reached over and held Mary's hand.

This wonderful miracle of grace has occurred thousands of times, as one has leaned on another, who leaned on God. Christianity is more caught than taught. When two begin walking hand-in-hand in faith,

Jesus Christ joins the relationship to perform miracles.

Jane — an angel to lean on — joins millions of others, who, masquerading as angels, provide shoulders to lean on, supported by Jesus. In the company of Him, who is constant and unfailing, miracles occur.

> *Trust in the Lord with all your heart*
> *and lean not on your own understanding;*
> *in all your ways acknowledge Him,*
> *and He will make your paths straight.*
>
> *Proverbs 3:5-6*

GOD'S NIGHT COOKIES

Like nearly everyone else, I'm a fan of *Peanuts*. I especially remember one episode that begins on a dark night with Snoopy sleeping on his dog house.

In the next frame Snoopy is kicking on the front door of the house as Charlie Brown looks out, sees him standing in the dark and queries, "Are you feeling lonely again?"

Charlie Brown lets Snoopy inside the house. Walking behind a discouraged looking Snoopy, Charlie Brown asks rhetorically, "It's a terrible feeling isn't it?"

The next frame shows them together in bed. Snoopy has the blanket pulled up under his chin as Charlie Brown continues counseling his depressed dog: "You wake up in the middle of the night all alone and everything seems hopeless."

Snoopy pulls the covers further up as Charlie continues: "You wonder what life is all about and why you're here, and does anyone really care, and you just stare into the dark and feel all alone."

In the final frame, Snoopy looks at Charlie Brown and longingly asks: "Do we have any night cookies?"

I suppose we've all had some dark nights when everything seems to be going wrong and we are longing for some of God's "night cookies."

I've had times like that in my life. Possibly you have also. Are you ever lonely? Afraid? Do you ever feel you're in a dog house? Your own? Or somebody else's? Maybe even God's?

At such times in my life, the Lord has always provided some marvelous "night cookies" of hope and encouragement. I'd like to share some of God's cookies that have helped me. May these examples encourage us when we have a dark night in some emotional dog house.

A few years ago, when Martha and I were on vacation in Hawaii, I would awaken early to meditate, think, and pray. Then I'd meander to a quaint pastry shop to drink coffee and read as I watched the sunrise over Diamond Head and Waikiki Beach.

What a wonderful experience to view the creation of a marvelous day in one of God's most beautiful places! Each new morning, the sky sported spectacular surprises from God's kaleidoscopic brush. The azure-shaded sea's gentle waves whispered His enduring love; the soft, snow-white sand — God's coverlet — offered comfort; the multihued birds soaring in the pacific breezes illustrated the easy strength of God's power; a few early swimmers and joggers reminded me of God's personal love for us all.

Those days, a treasure when recalled, always remind me of God's loving kindness and the marvelous words from *Psalm 136: 3-9,26:*

> *Give thanks to the Lord of lords...*
> *to him who alone does great wonders...*
> *who by his understanding made the heavens...*
> *who spread out the earth upon the waters...*
> *who made the great lights...*
> *the sun to govern the day...*
> *the moon and stars to govern the night...*
> *Give thanks to the God of heaven.*
> *His love endures forever.*

One Waikiki morning, having read *Psalm 136,* I suddenly realized how this marvelous *Psalm,* filled with great historical significance, embodied my Hawaiian experience. A liturgical ovation to the Lord as creator and as Israel's redeemer, the *Psalm* begins and ends with praise.

Psalm 136, sung regularly in Solomon's temple in times of worship, was the *Psalm* which the army of Jehoshaphat and the People of God sang as they marched to victory over their enemies. The *Psalm* has twenty-six verses. The first half of each verse declares something about God's creation, or His work in history. The end of each verse concludes with the recurring phrase: "His love endures forever." Twenty-six times we read, "His love endures forever!"

God seems to be working very hard to get something important across to us, namely that "His love endures forever!" God knows most of us are slow learners, and so He keeps repeating His truth time and time again. Twenty-six times in this one *Psalm!* If *Psalm 136* is not one of "God's night cookies," I never had one!

As a young preacher at Baylor University in the 1940's, I heard the evangelist B.B. Crimm preach on a number of occasions. Known as "Cowboy Crimm," because of his trademark, wide-brimmed, high-crowned Stetson, he was a most remarkable preacher, who, unfortunately, died in an automobile crash before he was universally known. Most of "Cowboy Crimm's" evangelistic crusades were in a big tent. His powerful voice and huge frame reflected a heart as big as Texas.

Brother Crimm once told about the time when, as a young preacher, he was called to pastor a church. Although he had never pastored, he felt God was leading him to this church, and he went.

The church's financial condition was abysmal because the members weren't giving much money. In an attempt to remedy the pecuniary problem, "Cowboy Crimm" preached his first sermon on the passage of Scripture from Malachi: "Will a man rob God?"

He preached twenty-one straight sermons on the same text: "Will a man rob God?" Every Sunday the congregation would hear the same text and the same sermon, over and over again — twenty-one times!

Finally, the deacons called on Brother Crimm and said, "Pastor, we appreciate your concern about stewardship, but we feel there are some other passages in the Bible which you might preach on occasionally."

"Cowboy Crimm" replied, "When you begin obeying this verse of scripture, then I'll move on to some others."

It wasn't long before Brother Crimm moved on — moved on to evangelistic work again, that is.

Brother Crimm may have been over-zealous, but, in one sense, there really is no point in moving on to the rest of the Bible until we have this basic twenty-six point sermon of *Psalm 136* embedded in our hearts, minds and lives. For until we comprehend that "His love endures forever," we'll never treasure the encouragement and hope the Bible offers; neither can we know the height nor depth nor breadth of His plan for our salvation.

"His love endures forever." What a wonderful message to comfort us when we awaken in the depth of a dark night feeling all alone as we wonder what life is all about and why we're here and if anyone really cares. In times of near despair we'll find the words, "His love endures forever," much more comforting than a dozen night cookies and a warm glass of milk.

Allow me to drive home the point regarding our Lord's enduring love. In *Isaiah 49: 15-16,* God asks and answers the question:

Can a mother forget the baby at her breast
and have no compassion on the child she has borne?

Though she may forget,
I will not forget you.

I fail to comprehend how a parent could ever forget a child. Could you forget your child? Could Martha forget? Could I forget my children and grandchildren? I couldn't forget them if I wanted to. They are embedded in me. They are an integral part of my life. There is absolutely no way I could forget them, or ever stop loving them!

Sadly, there are some parents who forget their children. We read of mothers killing their new-born. We know of mothers who disappear after leaving their children with the children's grandparents. Thousands of fathers have abandoned their children (and wives).

But God says that even if a mother can forget a child, He cannot and will not forget us! In *Isaiah 49:16,* God makes a unwavering statement of faithfulness:

I have engraved you on the palms of my hands.

George Adam Smith, the great Hebrew scholar, says the word "engraved" could best be translated as "tattooed." Remarkable! God has tattooed each of us on the palms of His hands!

Have you ever been to a tattoo parlor? I have, many times. I have gone, not to obtain a tattoo, but to puzzle over others who felt a tattoo would confirm their manhood. In 1943, after my seventeenth birthday, I enlisted in the Marine Corps. During my three-and-a-half years in the Corps including service with the Second Division's Sixth Regiment in Nagasaki, I watched many Marines voluntarily receive permanent markings. (You know there existed little opportunity for fun, when an off duty highlight involved visiting the local tattoo parlor.)

Several decades later, having reflected on *Isaiah 49:16:* "I have engraved you on the palms of my hands," I began to have questions concerning the nature of tattoos. I decided to do some research.

On a trip to Honolulu, I noticed a tattoo shop near our hotel. Wanting to do some serious Biblical research and, at the same time, desiring that my motives be conceived as pure, I asked Martha to go with me. Her initial shock indicated that she considered a tattoo parlor on the level of a house of ill repute.

After I picked Martha off the floor, I used my best Baptist oratory to convince her that tattoo parlors were legal and safe — relatively safe. Finally, she reluctantly agreed to accompany me, probably because she wanted evidence to complete commitment papers on me. Or perhaps she wanted to be able to defend me if a San Antonio television station produced a flash TV report: "Baptist Preacher Buckner Fanning Visits Honolulu Tattoo Parlor."

When we entered the tattoo parlor, we met the manager, a woman whose body was covered with tattoos. At least everything we could see was tattooed. The manager looked at me as if I were an escapee from an asylum when I told her who I was. Thankfully, Martha provided some credibility, and the manager's skepticism turned to enthusiastic support when I quoted *Isaiah 49:16* as the reason for my curiosity about tattoos.

This bright, young Swede shared a number of books and reference works on tattoos. We learned all we wanted to know about tattoos. For example, tattooing is an ancient art form dating back thousands of years. Surgery may remove most of a tattoo, but the surgical scar will remain. A skin graft fails to completely eliminate evidence of a tattoo because skin pigmentation cannot be accurately duplicated. Tattoos are as permanent as our physical features.

Then I asked, "What is the most sensitive part of the body to be tattooed?"

I thought the most sensitive area might be the face or some private part of the body. I was wrong. The most sensitive part of the human body to be tattooed is the palm of the hand and the top of the foot. I was amazed!

Suddenly, I understood more about what God was saying. His word was fantastic. God tattoos our name upon the palms of His hands and there is no way He can forget us — no way He can erase us from His hands. We are forever one with Him, and in Him. A spiritual explosion erupted in my mind as the crucifixion of Jesus took on a new and deeper significance!

When Jesus was nailed to the cross they "tattooed" Him with nails in His hands and in His feet — the most sensitive parts of His body. The scars from those wounds would never be erased.

A few days after the crucifixion and resurrection, when the disciple, Thomas, "Doubting Thomas," saw those scars in the hands of the resurrected Christ, he exclaimed, "My Lord and my God."

Thomas saw those scars as the ineradicable sign of God's enduring love for him — a love that lasts forever!

What Thomas came to know, we can know! If we, like Thomas, need help in overcoming our doubting moments, we can recall the "tattoos" of Jesus and know that each of us is engraved on the palm of God's hands. Those recollections provide a "night cookie" that will bring us through the darkest hours of life, for "His love endures forever!"

Back at the hotel coffee shop on the beach, reading that scripture and recalling our experience in the tattoo shop the day before, my spirit was lifted and my faith renewed in an indescribable way. I had one of God's "night cookies" served with my morning coffee that day.

Something totally unexpected occurred. The young woman who had been serving me coffee each morning came to my table and asked me if I wanted a refill?

We'd gotten to know each other on a friendly, first-name basis. She knew I was a Christian pastor, and wanted to talk.

She said, "Buckner, I have three sons. My first husband and I divorced a number of years ago, and I recently remarried and now have a wonderful home and a happy marriage. In my previous marriage, I had two sons and was expecting our third child, when two months before the baby was born, my husband left us. A few months later we divorced."

She paused and hesitantly said, "I've been having a challenge with my third son. He is now sixteen years old. He came to me recently and asked if he were illegitimate."

She replied to her son, "Of course not! You're not illegitimate! Your father and I were married and did not divorce until after you were born. No, you're not illegitimate! Why do you ask?"

She described how her son told her that he'd felt this way all of his life. When he was much younger, his older brothers, and some of the kids at school, had called him a "bastard." He began to cry when he told his mother, "I thought I was illegitimate. I've thought it for years."

The waitress cried also when she told how she took her sixteen year-old boy in her arms and said, "Son, you're not a bastard. You're not illegitimate. Even if you were, you wouldn't be any less loved by me."

Her story touched me deeply. I stood. Putting my arms around her, I said, "You're a wonderful mother, and God gave you the right words to say to your hurting son. I also know that your words changed his heart and mind forever."

She began crying quietly, and gently said, "Yes, he's been different ever since."

Who wouldn't be different after hearing that? Who wouldn't feel the sunrise on a beautiful beach beginning a new day with a God-filled future after a statement like that? Every discouraged Snoopy in the world would feel better after hearing that "night cookie."

Yes — "God's love endures forever." He's tattooed our names on His hands!

Everyone who's ever been in the doghouse of despondency will feel better after hearing these words! Every person who's ever felt they didn't belong, or weren't loved or wanted, would feel better after hearing that!

Jesus came into the world to personally reveal God's enduring love for all of us. He came to say to all who've felt like bastards, or dogs, or rejects, or outsiders, or unwanted — "I love you. My love endures forever."

Our three-dimensional minds cannot comprehend infinity. Our heads spin when we try to imagine "forever." Can we even begin to realize how long forever is? Listen — it's forever!

The love of God and the kindness of God are combined into one magnificent word — lovingkindness. The word, lovingkindness, is combined in one life — the life of Jesus — who then combines His life with ours and tattoos our names on His hands. Forever!

You can't beat a night cookie like that! Take the cookie, crawl in beside Snoopy and Charlie Brown, pull up the covers, and close your eyes. Rest in the Lord. You are literally in His hands, His feet, His heart — forever. He's got your name tattooed there — forever!

So sleep tight tonight...and every night.

Every time you see someone with a tattoo, let those body marks remind you that God, too, has engraved your name on the palms of His hands!

AN ARTIST FOR ALL TIMES: YEA! GLORY! HALLELUJAH!

When Lisa, our daughter, was nine years old, she would often sit with a dear friend of ours in church, while I led the worship service and Martha sang in the choir. One memorable Sunday, Lisa, a gifted child artist, sketched a picture of the service on the back of the Sunday bulletin.

Behind my full-length figure, right hand pointed heavenward and left hand cradling a beautiful leather-bound black Bible, stood the regally-robed choir, all smiling broadly. On the left side of the choir, she had drawn the United States flag that stands in the sanctuary; on the right, she drew the Christian flag. Lisa, for some unaccountable reason, had portrayed each flag blowing inward. Perhaps our air conditioner created weird currents of which I am unaware. In the background, Lisa had sketched our beautiful picture window. Discounting parental prejudice, her artwork rivaled the best realism of Norman Rockwell.

Following the service, as Lisa shared her drawing with me, my eyes were initially attracted to the beautiful smiles of the choir. No one ever frowned in Lisa's childhood drawings, reflecting, perhaps, God's wish that we "be joyful always" and "content in all things."

Next, my handsome face, curly hair flowing, penetrating eyes, and a soft smile, attracted my attention. "Yes," I said to myself, "that's the way I really look. Cameras and mirrors fail to give my engaging face the justice it deserves. What a realistic artist my child is!!!"

Seriously, aren't we encouraged by those who help us look and do better than we actually feel we are! God bless them all.

(A pause for preaching here: I hope you view yourself as handsome or beautiful, for in God's eyes, you truly are. The Bible promises that in Heaven our physical bodies will be made perfect, reflecting a loving and pure spirit. On earth, too, our spirit, more than our physical appearance, determines our attractiveness. Because we tend to look the way we feel — be joyful, cultivate peace, develop enthusiasm!!! Please understand: God abhors vanity. Waste no minutes on narcissism. Life is too short to spend time in front of the mirror bemoaning your deficiencies. Simply look as good as you can and be joyful! Cultivate an enthusiastic, peaceful spirit that allows God's love to shine through your physical appearance.)

Lisa's drawing reflected my parenthetical words. Extending from my mouth, Lisa had drawn a line leading to a cartoon style cloud, circling these words: "God loves you and that's no joke!"

In a similar fashion, from the mouths of eight or nine people in the choir came the words, "Amen," and from others, "Yea."

"Yea!" I like that. I believe it's better than "Amen."

"Yea!" seems more fitting for us by better representing the energy and enthusiasm that characterized the early Christians. At times, our modern day "Amen" sounds somber — as if only those with theological degrees wearing floor length black robes can intone this sacrosanct word with proper decorum. We would do well to remember that Biblical "Amens" compare to our enthusiastic cheers. Yea! Glory! Hallelujah!

A sketch of the stained glass window behind our choir dominated Lisa's drawing, just as it dominates our sanctuary. The stained glass window, the visual focal point of our sanctuary, is a thirty-foot by twenty-foot rendition of the resurrected Christ ascending, with arms outstretched to the world, as figures of loving people reach up to Him, artistically interpreting Jesus when He said, "And if I be lifted up from the earth, I will draw all men to me."

From the smiling mouth of Jesus, Lisa had drawn a line connecting to a cartoon-like circle containing, in huge letters, the word, "AMEN!"

Lisa's artwork profoundly touched my soul, making me grateful for children who have resplendent, loving impressions of Jesus and the church. What an inspirational picture then! What a marvelous picture today! What a beautiful promise for tomorrow! That hopeful illustration, one of my cherished possessions, continues to hang prominently in my office.

After admiring Lisa's picture, I handed the sketch to Martha who agreed that we had raised a child prodigy, a Mozart of artists. Martha complimented Lisa on her spectacular creation. Then, leaning close to me, she whispered, "Buckner, when Jesus says 'Amen' to your preaching, you are really preaching!"

True! I'm convinced that we preachers, to have any confidence at all, certainly must always be assured of God's presence with us. At the same time, I am fully persuaded that when we proclaim His love, then our God shouts a resounding "Yea," that reverberates like comforting thunder from one end of the universe to the other! And that's no joke!

God is no grouch. No kill-joy. No wet blanket. In contrast to the devil, who takes pleasure in our pain — who rejoices in our suffering — God desires an abundantly rich life for us all. Jesus came that we might "have life, and have it to the full" (*John 10:10*).

Because God granted us free will, tragedy can occur. I am convinced, however, that God is always for us. God's overflowing forgiveness, love and guidance enables us to rejoice. Yea! Glory! Hallelujah!

Even when tragedy strikes, Christians can be assured that "in all things God works for the good of those who love him" (*Romans 8:28*).

As children, many of us memorized, before any others, the verse from *John 3:16:*

For God so loved the world that He gave His one and only Son,
that whoever believes in him shall not perish but have eternal life.

Some negative folks I know neglect the next equally important verse which promises God's fidelity:

For God did not send His Son into the world to condemn the world,
but to save the world through Him.

Do you know those nabobs of negativism who feel that God sent them into the world to condemn it? Instead of fretting over them, remember what God told Job's friends (*Job 38:2*):

Who is this that darkens my counsel
with words without knowledge?

God sent Jesus into the world to reveal His unconditional love for each of us. Jesus gives us the message: "God loves you and that's no joke!"

He loves us even if we refuse to love Him. God is love, whether we believe Him or doubt Him, whether we accept Him or reject Him. God has been, is, and always will be, love.

Love, the great equalizer, shows no favorite. God loves the most moral, church-going person equally with the most immoral, venomous individual. God's love, a gift given unearned, blesses all who receive it. A gift, earned, ceases to be a gift.

God declares He has given the gift of love to all who accept Him. The unearned package of God's love is available for all to open. He has given all of His love to each one of us — to you!

God does not love all of us! That is no typographical error. It's true. God does not love all of us! He loves *each* one of us! Separately, apart from everybody else in all the universe, He loves you.

If you had been the only person in all the world who ever failed or sinned or made a mistake or became discouraged or were harmed by others, Jesus would have come into the world, been crucified and resurrected from the grave just for you! He did everything just to show you His love. He forgives you of your selfish thoughts and actions that prevented you from experiencing love, joy, and peace. And that's no joke.

Jesus would have been born in Bethlehem, would have ministered in Galilee, performed miracles, taught in parables, died on a cross, been resurrected from the dead and would come to you personally with His message of salvation even if you had been the only individual in all the world who needed forgiveness! As Augustine said, "He loves each of us as though there is only one to love."

Yea! Glory! Hallelujah!

You and I tend to love conditionally. God loves unconditionally.

Our human type of love says, "I'll love you if you love me, do as I desire, live as I live, act in ways that I approve."

God's unconditional love says, "I love you in sickness or in health, in wealth or in poverty, in gentleness or in hate, in humility or in pride, in trust or in unbelief, in joy or in grief, in peace or in fretfulness."

Why? Because God's grace, more than a hymn, is amazing. God's love is incomprehensible.

Let me explain God's love in a way that parents can understand. Martha and I had been married for seven years before our first child,

Michael, was born. Our first baby died at birth. Later Martha had a miscarriage. Because of these heart-breaking experiences, Michael's birth turned our disappointment and despair into joy incapable of being described.

Three years later, Stephen's birth gave us ecstasy equal to Michael's birth. Two boys! Wonderful! When Steve was born, we didn't say to Michael: "Mike, we have good news and bad news. The good news is you have a little brother. The bad news is that your mother and I have to divide our love so we can give Steve his share. Because we must divide our love, you now get fifty percent. That's the only fair thing to do, isn't it? After all, we are dividing our love equally."

Six years later, to the thrill and delight of us all, Lisa was born! When that wonderful event occurred, we did not say to Mike and Steve, "Boys, we have some good news and some bad news. The good news is you have a little sister, and the bad news is that our love will be divided into thirds for each of you. Because we only have one hundred percent of love to divide, we are doing the fair thing and giving each of you an equal share. We are equal opportunity parents."

When we begin looking at love in this way, we see how ludicrous conditional love would be, how totally impossible! Unconditional love is indivisible. When love is involved, each receives one hundred percent. Unconditional love doesn't come in fractions.

When love is involved, each child is an only child! At certain times or under certain conditions, we may approve of the behavior of one child more than the others. Love, however, remains one hundred percent. Martha and I love each child as an only child. That's the way God regards you. You are God's only child. Celebrate His love!

If we, as sinful human beings, can love our children with all our hearts and souls, how much more does the Divine Being, the eternal, infinite, unconditionally-loving Heavenly Father, love you — love each of us? One hundred percent of God's love is an infinite, incomprehensible number. God loves you and that's no joke!

Thank you Lord for loving me.

Thank you Lisa for reminding me.

Yea! Glory! Hallelujah!

SURPRISED BY JOY

Good news seldom makes the front page. Bad news sells newspapers. Good news becomes relegated to the classified section so customers will focus on the ads. I made this observation a few years ago when I stumbled across an amazing article in one of the back pages of our newspaper — the section containing ads for water softeners, magic-markers, fertilizers, and that sort of thing.

On a "filler page," a small headline grabbed my attention: "Became Clown For Son's Sake." The Associated Press story out of Rochester, New York, read as follows:

Richard T. McAllister of Rochester says he decided to become a circus clown recently because he wanted his 12-year-old son, Michael, to learn to accept laughter. Michael is a midget. "He would hide because he thought people were laughing at him," his father said. "Since he joined me in my act, he's become a big ham."

This article communicated a powerful message which said volumes in a few words. Because Michael was small, he hid. He was afraid. The ridicule from others drained joy and laughter from his life. Congenital circumstances caused Michael's confidence to hover around the red-zone empty line.

Most of us, from time to time, have found our confidence gauge dipping below empty. This complex world presents colossal problems that drain us. We feel like midgets trying to push an out-of-gas SUV.

Instead of refueling, we complain: "Here I am — one little person in a complex world, a world of big money, big power, big influence. I'm too tiny to defend myself or contend with powerful people."

Negative people have no emotional fuel for laughter. They feel like "Midget Michael." Depleted of joy and laughter, they search for ways to compensate for their perceived inadequacies.

Some surrender their lives to side-of-the-road living. Others become outrageously flamboyant hoping to divert attention from their emptiness. Still others refuel with alcohol or drugs. Many use sex, sleep, work, hobbies or recreational pursuits to compensate for the empty feelings.

The Bible tells us (and Jesus came in person to "show and tell" us) how much God loves us totally and completely just as we are. The Bible repeatedly tells us we would be more joyful if we rid ourselves of jealousy, envy and inadequate feelings.

Television, movies, and magazines want to convince us otherwise. The advertising agencies use powerful propaganda attempting to make us feel inadequate and unloved. Televison, radio, billboards, newspapers, and magazines overflow with messages indicating our incompetence and smallness.

Advertisers want us to feel empty. Their message? More is never enough. Bigger is insufficient. Thin is too fat. Wealth can be found in just a little more. Love is only a new toothpaste away. Bliss is the next vacation.

Logic tells us that our nation offers us more than any civilization has ever possessed. Our emotions, stimulated by advertising propaganda, make us feel we're being cheated out of opportunities. Everyone else is doing better, having more fun, experiencing less discomfort.

Caught in this dilemma, how can we change? Can we change, or has the media captured our hearts and our minds and made us willing slaves to all that is "new," "better," or "faster?"

In addition to advertising propaganda, many situations can make us feel small and inadequate. I'm persuaded, however, that we must comprehend the power the media has over our minds if we have hope to look beyond worldly desires, because worldly temptations will leave us empty to spiritual promises that will make life truly meaningful.

Do not love the world or anything in the world.
If anyone loves the world, the love of the Father is not in him.
For everything in the world —
the cravings of sinful man, the lust of the eyes and the boasting
of what he has and does —
comes not from the Father but from the world.
The world and its desires pass away,
but the man who does the will of God lives forever.

I John 2: 15-17

We — each of us — may feel small and inadequate for any number of a hundred reasons, logical and illogical. I, at times, become discouraged. Sometimes, the trials and troubles of the world seem insurmountable, but it is a comforting reminder to know that the human part of Jesus, too, may have, on occasion, felt overwhelmed:

When He saw the crowds, He had compassion on them,
because they were harassed and helpless,
like sheep without a shepherd.
Then He said to His disciples,
"The harvest is plentiful but the workers are few.
Ask the Lord of the harvest, therefore,
to send out workers into His harvest field."

Matthew 9:36-38

When we begin to feel small and insignificant, we can, of course, turn to our loving and powerful God, remembering that we can do all things when strengthened by Him. We can also allow the example of the little boy from Rochester, a camouflaged angel, to inspire us to look heavenward.

What did Michael have? What changed his attitude? A father who loved him! His father loved Michael in words, in actions and in deeds. Michael's father demonstrated his love three ways: He changed his job; he changed his clothes; and he joined the "act" with his son.

Every one of us — whether we are little or big, good or bad, simple or smart — have exactly the same kind of Father. God, our loving, heavenly Father, has done and is doing for us exactly what Michael's father did for him.

God loves us. He loves you. He loves me. He loves everyone! He loves you as if you were the only person in all the world who needed love.

Our Heavenly Father, the creator, is also the sustainer. God was and is with us. Two thousand years ago He worked in a carpenter shop, supplied wine for wedding parties, healed the sick, accepted the unacceptable, and berated the sanctimonious who made religion and rules more important than relationships.

He remains with us — twenty-four hours a day, each and every day — working miracles that often go unrecognized. He's an amazing carpenter, constructing foundations, windows, doors, and steeples without charge for anyone who asks Him. Where there is sorrow, He brings joy; sickness — health; rejection — acceptance; hypocrisy — right living. You will know Him by His actions.

He's obsessed with giving joy to all the "little Michaels" in the world. In the New Testament, we read the word, "joy," or a synonym like merriment, or celebration, two hundred and seventy-eight times!

Think of it! God tells us two hundred and seventy-eight times that He wants us to celebrate life. He came in person — and remains in spirit — to bring joy to our daily "act" of living. He makes an ordinary day extraordinary; the mundane, magnificent; the common, commendable.

When we feel loved at the time we are most unlovable, joy surprises us. Jesus told of the young man who, rebellious and immature, wanted freedom to live as he pleased. When his father prematurely gave the young man his demanded inheritance, he traveled to another country where he squandered his fortune in wild living. Impoverished and starving, he decided to return home to ask his father for forgiveness and request a job as a hired hand on the family farm. Expecting rejection and recrimination, the young man was surprised by joy when his father celebrated his return (*Luke 15: 20-24*):

...his father saw him and was filled with compassion for him;
he ran to his son, threw his arms around him and kissed him.
The son said to him,
"Father, I have sinned against heaven and against you.
I am no longer worthy to be called your son."
But the father said to the servants,
"Quick! Bring the best robe and put it on him
Put a ring on his finger and sandals on his feet.
Bring the fatted calf and kill it.
Let's have a feast and celebrate.
For this son of mine was dead and is alive again,
he was lost and is found."

Our God is a God of celebrations. We, too, can be surprised by joy. While we may avoid responsibility and commitment that interferes with our selfish desires, God patiently waits for our return to Him.

Our humble and contrite acceptance of God's love makes all heaven applaud, and turns our life into an eternal celebration.

Little Michael learned to laugh because his father became a clown. A clown! Think of it! Clowns, by puncturing pompous and pious people, make children of us all. Laughter, the great equalizer, brings all of us together.

Rodeo clowns are my favorite, because they remind me of Jesus. In addition to bringing joy, rodeo clowns serve as life-savers. When a cowboy is thrown by a bronco or bull, the clown is there to divert the attention of the dangerous animal. The clown draws the focus of the bucking bronco with his flying hoofs and the Brahma bull with his dangerous horns. As the angry animal chases the clown, the fallen rider escapes to safety.

Jesus diverts the flying hoofs of evil and the piercing horns of death away from us. He sacrificed His life so we can escape to safety. That's certainly something worthy of celebration!

Richard said his son Michael became a "big ham." From a little boy to a big ham. Michael overcame his preoccupation with his handicap by helping others laugh. He was no longer inhibited, self-conscious and worried about what others thought or said. He experienced freedom from self-pity by bringing joy to others.

But I must tell you the rest of the story, for it's a real zinger. There was a one-sentence concluding paragraph in the newspaper story. Here it is: *Richard McAllister, 39, got a four-month leave of absence from his job as a carpenter and joined a show now touring New Jersey.*

Michael's father was a carpenter! Does that shake your mind and touch your heart? A carpenter! Michael's father was a carpenter!

Mine, too. And yours.

Our Father worked as a carpenter in a place called Nazareth, two thousand years ago. As carpenter of eternal values, He understands how things are made, how they break and how they can be repaired. He knows how to lay a solid foundation and how to build a structure to withstand the winds of life. Your carpenter, and mine, can repair broken hearts and hopes. He can return our demolished lives to new structures.

Like Michael's father, our Father, the carpenter, changed his job and his clothes to become involved in our lives — to act with us — helping us live with joy and love and self-esteem.

Jesus builds, repairs and brings celebration to lives. He's quite a carpenter — and a Father — who surprises us with joy.

MEN IN BLACK

Soon after the birth of our third child, Lisa, Martha and I made a commitment to concentrate our marriage on building memories for our family. We decided to spend as many of our vacations as possible in Hawaii, where we could find relief from the incessant demands created by extremely busy schedules without interruptions breaching our time together. (Message to young pastors and, indeed, to all whose time seems ceaselessly besieged: Take your vacations where you and your family can give each other undivided attention.)

We have spent some magnificent times together in a large beach house that basks in God's glorious sunshine on the North Shore of Oahu, Hawaii. What a blessing and joy to share time with those you love most — a growing family (growing spiritually and in numbers) — in one of God's most wondrous earthly locations, the legendary homeland of the Polynesians!

Not so long ago by time's measure, but before our family had grown to its current number, our three young children were swimming and sunning on a Waikiki beach while Martha and I enjoyed the shade of a broad, colorful umbrella as we read, relaxed and shared time together. What a pleasure to recall those simple days when the hours rolled by as serenely as gentle waves undulating toward a peaceful shore. Pure delight!

Suddenly, our tranquil day was interrupted by a voice crying in the distance. Martha and I looked toward the shrill bellowing and saw, about a hundred yards down the beach, a man walking toward us.

At first, his voice was like the distant howling of a distressed animal and he appeared as an indistinct black dot plodding slowly along the ivory sand amidst frolicking bathers dressed in colorful swim wear. Even at a distance, he looked quite out of place.

He carried no umbrella, and was obviously sweltering under the sun. Except for his white shirt that, as he approached, I could see was soaked with moisture, he was dressed in black. His black suit seemed to pinch the blood from his face and the thin black tie enhanced his mournful appearance. His black shoes appeared to harness his movement as he trudged along the beach holding an enormous black Bible above his head with his left hand as he pointed accusingly with his right index finger.

As he approached, I could tell he was a nice looking, but frustrated looking young man, in the prime of life. This young man, filled with hate and vindictiveness, spewed like a volcano, accusing everyone — young and old — of being horrendous sinners, as we simply were enjoying a wonderful family time.

Holding the Bible aloft he shouted words of angry denunciation and condemnation to us all. Both his words and body language dripped with fiery judgmentalism. This was no actor, no wrestler promoting attendance for the next event, no preacher trying to muster a crowd for the night's tent meeting. This man was furious.

As I listened to his fiery damnations, I tried to imagine what was going on inside him. What motivated his behavior? I know one thing for certain, he was sincere. Give him credit for that.

He had courage. I know it takes courage to preach on the street, for I've done it many times in my years in evangelism. I've preached from flat-bed trucks on courthouse squares on Saturday afternoons, and I've preached on the street in some unfriendly places, such as Bourbon Street in New Orleans. While preaching, I've heard plenty of scoffers and hecklers. Consequently, I could appreciate the courage of the man in black, but his angry and hostile spirit did no one, including himself, any good because, for whatever reason, he was extremely angry at everybody, perhaps beginning with himself. We don't know. However, the love of God was not expressed either vocally or visually — and lots of folks would have "soaked up" that wonderful message of God's love like the sunshine itself.

Failing to understand that joy and recreation are natural desires to be directed and controlled in positive ways, the young man in black endeavored to transfer his own feelings of anger about himself onto others. He reminded me of the experience Jesus had with His disciples that was described in *Luke 9:51-56*.

The Samaritans would not allow Jesus to come into their city because He was heading for Jerusalem, and when the disciples, James and John, saw this, they asked, "Lord, do you want us to call fire down from Heaven to destroy them?" (*Luke 9:54*).

Jesus rebuked them because of their hostile attitude.

We will do well to understand that the early disciples, rather than being old men with long beards and decrepit bodies, were robust young men. Dr. Hershey Davis, an outstanding New Testament scholar of a generation ago, determined from extensive research that the disciples were all in the prime of life. (Peter and Matthew may have been the oldest of the group.)

Jesus sought younger men as his disciples because He knew that His ministry was going to be cut short by the cross, and He wanted vigorous men — young minds (and bodies) that were open, pliable, enthusiastic, dedicated, and energetic — to carry the Gospel to the ends of the earth.

In the passage from Luke, we read how a youthful attitude can also generate disadvantages. James and John, on fire with enthusiasm, wanted to destroy people who rejected the message of Jesus. Rather than obliterate people, Jesus sought to transform people by His love for them. Later, John became known as the Apostle of Love, because he finally caught the spirit of Jesus.

The disposition to destroy people, to judge and condemn, comes from an immaturity that has failed to be saturated with the loving spirit of Christ that receives people irrespective of their actions and attitudes. Those who have experienced little pain and suffering, those who have traveled a short distance on the road of life, sometimes fail to comprehend the power of love and forgiveness to transform people. Young people, therefore, may tend to be more critical of others for the feelings they themselves have.

Many of us have heard preachers at one time or another speak on the subject of hell as if they were glad people were going there. Why rejoice in a sinner's damnation? Why be angry when people reject God? Rejection of the peace that passes all understanding should, I think, make us sad, not glad. The men in black — those who denounce all of us as "Sons and daughters of Sodom and Gomorrah" — seem to enjoy damning us.

I surveyed the people around this particular man in black trying to see whom he might be addressing. There were no wild parties, drunken orgies or immoral acts taking place. I only saw some tourists having fun enjoying a typical afternoon at the beach. I don't doubt that among those frolickers there were some who were "like sheep without a shepherd," but I didn't see anyone on the fast track to hell.

Apparently, the man in black had determined that we were all bound for hell, and he was just plain angry. I never had the opportunity to talk with this young man, but based on other men in black whom I have known, I believe that he equated happiness and pleasure with sin. His angry vituperations seemed to indicate, "Because you are having fun, you are a sinner, and I am mad because I can't have fun, too."

Men in black seem to be determined that hell is our destiny for the "sin" of enjoying God's gift of life. How sad.

Unfortunately, there are more than a few men in black — well-meaning but misdirected Christians — who believe fun and pleasure come from the devil. This belief is unsound theology, but, sadly, some clergy follow this dead-end path, especially in their impressionable years of ministry. Have they not read that Jesus promised us love, joy, peace and an abundant life?

When I review my years as a preacher, I realize that in the early days of my ministry, I had some "touches" of this judgmental attitude revealed in some of my sermons and discussions. As a twenty-year-old former Marine, I had been exposed to much more sin and violence than love and joy. I tended, therefore, to be more judgmental then.

Auspiciously and providentially, God brought people and books into my life that helped me see the "good" in the Good News. I was enabled to celebrate God's unconditional love that frees us from the letter of the law. My experiences helped me understand that *Amazing Grace* is much more than a song. I was very sincere, then and now, but I had to learn from personal experience, and the leadership of the Holy Spirit, that no amount of sincerity ever justifies a judgmental spirit or an angry attitude.

Unfortunately, there are a few well-meaning, sincere preachers who perpetuate the false idea that fun is automatically sinful and that Jesus came into the world as a divine wet blanket and a champion kill-joy.

How tragic it is to portray Jesus, the world's great joy-giver, in such a distorted way.

I've wondered if this propensity to negativism and masochism was fostered by the spiritually heretical and emotionally unhealthy concept that somehow we're better Christians if we suffer rather than celebrate. Whatever the cause, this pernicious idea persists, poisoning the world. There is no truth to the idea that to be a "good" Christian one must be consistently negative, personally obnoxious, vocally judgmental, and specialize in spreading doom and gloom to everyone.

I'm eternally grateful to have grown up in a healthy and happy Christian home in which I was given a positive and loving impression about Jesus. In my early ministry when I encountered the men in black — the tribe of unhealthy, unhappy prognosticators of doom and gloom — I was saved from the disease by some loving friends, caring professors and encouraging mentors.

As I continued reading and studying the New Testament, I kept finding Jesus enjoying time with sinners, publicans, prostitutes, tax collectors, lepers and the other outsiders of His day. His informal and down to earth manner with everyone helped me understand that Christianity favors the common man and woman. Christ talked with people on a first-name basis. He even nicknamed some of his followers.

When we let our minds and spirits soak in the New Testament, we begin to catch the feeling of the healthy, happy, wholesome relationship Jesus had with people. We catch what C.S. Lewis calls the "good infection" or perhaps, it begins to "catch us," when we realize that Jesus began his public ministry not in a cemetery, but at a celebration in Cana of Galilee where He turned water to wine! The "good infection" catches us when we understand that Jesus invites us all, without exception, to a party!

Years ago at Laity Lodge, the outstanding retreat center in the Texas hill country, I heard Carl Olson speak. He helped me immeasurably, and his marvelous book, *Come To The Party,* is a book I reread often.

Carl both said and wrote something that I have never forgotten. "There are some people who fail to recognize there's a party going on. Some people know there's a party going on, but they don't believe they are invited. Others know a party is going on and they know they're invited, but they don't believe they deserve to go. Still others know they're invited, know they can attend and stay because they've been invited by the Host!"

It took me a while, but I finally joined the fourth group. Yes — He really does invite us all to a party!

Reading the Gospels convinced me that a drinking, cursing, fighting sailor by the name of Simon Peter would not have followed some negative, life-hating, judgmental individual. Nor can I, in the wildest stretch of my imagination, conceive of those teen-age brothers, James and John, whom Jesus nicknamed "Sons of Thunder," following anyone less than a man who exploded with life, love and hope. Jesus proclaimed that he had come to give life and to give it to us abundantly.

I had to learn from experience that "religion" can't give life! Never! In fact, it produces death. If religion produced life, the world would have experienced it long ago, because religion produces a spreading virus of rules, creeds, customs and ceremonies to which mankind has been exposed for thousands of years. Religious rules and regulations regurgitate death, not life.

We're sadly mistaken if we feel, that by observing man-made rules and regulations, we can somehow produce new life within us. Following this path of rules and regulations will doom us forever to the treadmill of religion. Religious rules can no more make a person a Christian than sleeping in a garage can make him an automobile.

When we accept God's unconditional love, and experience the joyful life He gives, we will be completely transformed by Christ. Our attitude about God, life, and the world will be revolutionized.

To drive that point home, let me tell you more about the man in black on the beaches of Waikiki. As we sat on the beach, watching and listening to the preacher's vilification, we suddenly noticed a dramatic and frightening event taking place in the ocean behind the evangelist. Had he turned around, he would have seen a captivating drama occurring about a hundred yards offshore.

Suddenly, angels masquerading as lifeguards, sprang into action and moved quickly toward some panicky commotion among the surfers and swimmers out in the ocean. The surf was rough that day and the lifeguards were paddling their surf boards with great difficulty toward the scene of the confusion. A swimmer was in trouble. He was literally in "over his head" and about to drown. The lifeguards finally reached the dying man, lifted his limp body onto a surfboard and then, in rough water, with much physical effort and courage, brought him to shore, placed him on the sand, and began performing CPR.

All eyes were riveted on the scene of salvation, as the man in black continued to shout aspersions in ever-increasing strident tones. As the evangelist preached, we "Sons and Daughters of Sodom and Gomorrah" prayed. We were all thrilled when the dying swimmer began to respond. The lifeguards continued working feverishly until an ambulance arrived and rushed him to a hospital from where we later learned of his recovery. He had been saved!

As we walked back to our places on the beach, our man in black, who had never stopped denouncing us, continued his fiery condemnations unabated. He totally missed the act of unselfish love and raw courage displayed by the lifeguards, who had saved a sinking, desperate, frightened man.

This event, indelibly etched on my mind by contrasting examples, remains as a constant reminder of the kind of person I want Christ to help me be. I pray that I will always be a man who brings the joyful news of life everlasting, and ask that He allow me to live the abundant life He has promised us all. May I spread the "good infection" of joy and peace to everyone I meet!

Periodically all of us need to be reminded of our sins, failures and frailties, for we all have them. We must remember that though we have not all sinned alike, all alike have sinned. We ask to be drawn to that joyful day when we were all "in over our heads," drowning in the engulfing waves of disobedience, and were rescued by God's loving and courageous "Lifeguard," Jesus Christ our Savior!

Why did Jesus have to do this to save us? Why didn't He teach us how to swim so we would never go under; never fail; never sin? To have prevented our capacity to sin, He would have had to create us with built-in life preservers. But to do this would have forced Him to contradict His own nature: He had created us in His image which means that we have the power of choice.

So what did He do? Rather than make us float above the deep waters of sin, He got into the water with us. He rescued us by personally taking all our sin and literally going under — going down beneath the waves of death and emerging victorious — thereby saving us by taking our place. God did this for us through His son — the

Living Lifeguard — who died and rose again to bring us safely ashore.

As Paul declared, "He has swallowed up death in victory." Death, that was swallowing us up and dragging us down into the dark and frightening depths, was swallowed by Christ so that we might be rescued, redeemed, saved!

I pray that somewhere along the beach of life the men in black come to know the joy of the Lord and the love of God.

All of us would do well to remember Martin Luther's admonition that the Bible is read forward but understood backward. We are to begin at the end, the resurrection, for without this message, the Bible will never make sense. If we begin with ourselves, or with the shackles of a religious life, our life story becomes "A tale told by an idiot, full of sound and fury, signifying nothing."

To paraphrase T.S. Eliot, in every beginning there is an end, and in every end there is a beginning. When we read the end of the Bible, we see that the end is the beginning. The death and resurrection of Christ was planned before the foundation of the world!

Looking back to that day at Waikiki Beach, I'm reminded of my own experience. When I struggled in deep water trying to save myself from going under, I cried for help, and was lifted from the depths by the love and grace of God. He rescued me.

Because of my blessed experience, I'm serving with many others who have shared the same "amazing grace," and we are helping each other to be God's lifeguards, always reaching out to those who are about to go under. Our shout to everyone on the beaches of life resounds with the word of resurrection, not denunciation; resuscitation, not condemnation!

I was sinking deep in sin,
Far from the peaceful shore,
Very deeply stained within,
Sinking to rise no more;
But the Master of the Sea
Heard my despairing cry,
From the waters lifted me,
Now safe am I.
Love lifted me! Love lifted me!
When nothing else could help,
Love lifted me.

ANGELS KEEP ON DANCING

"There's No Business Like Show Business," especially when performed by children — ESPECIALLY — when rendered by your own grandchildren!

Our clan — all twelve of us — including children and grandchildren, were enjoying a vacation in a rented house on the beach in Haleiwa, Hawaii. While there, a family performance, that, in our view, supplanted an Academy Award production, took place. But first some background.

With the birth of our first grandchild, Avery, I began a tradition that has continued with our other grandchildren, Julia, Meagan, and Michael, Jr., and endures to this day. I wrap my arms around each child, softly say, "I love you," and then I sing:

You are my sunshine, my only sunshine.
You make me happy when skies are gray.
You'll never know dear how much I love you.
Please don't take my sunshine away.

While singing I pray silently that my monotone will inspire each child to musical heights unimpaired by my poor performance. Anyone who has heard me sing will testify that my enthusiasm for music supersedes, by 120 decibels, my singing talent. Perhaps the psalmist had me in mind when he wrote, "Make a joyful noise." Nonetheless, my grandchildren have learned the words of "You Are My Sunshine" from me, the tune they've discovered elsewhere.

As most grandparents have joyfully experienced, Martha and I have been renamed by our grandchildren. Avery, our first grandchild, called Martha "Mimi" and she named me, "Beau." Our other grandchildren picked up on the names that have spread to our grandchildren's contemporaries and many of our close friends. We like our new names which seem to give us a feeling of freedom from all sorts of cares and responsibilities. Those frolicsome names remind us that, in God's eyes, we all are children for whom He wants joy and peace to abound.

Grandchildren seem to give grandparents an earthly renewal. We become more playful, more forgiving, more attentive than we were with our own children when, filled with personal ambition, we attempted to balance work demands and worship with parenting and friendships. Perhaps God inspires the grandchildren to give us names that reflect that joyful, trusting nature.

Now back to the production in Haleiwa, Hawaii. One evening after the family had returned from a delightful meal at "Pizza Bob's," all four of our grandchildren were in our bedroom, tickling and wrestling one another. Suddenly, we all burst into song, singing, "You Are My Sunshine." This spontaneous outburst spurred one of the children to shout, "Let's put on a show and sing our song," a suggestion enthusiastically endorsed by all.

We began preparing for the performance. I notified the others who began rearranging the living room into a small theater, while Mimi, a trained musician and popular performer, began rehearsing with the children.

As excitement for the performance grew, the children decided to dress Hawaiian style. The adult sized, colorful Hawaiian shirts they put on reached the floor. Mimi draped their necks with artificial leis and pinned flowers in their hair. Except for all the blond hair, light complexions and blue eyes, the children had been transformed into authentic Hawaiians.

After rehearsing several times, the children were about to perform when four-year-old Meagan, who had been taking ballet, spontaneously exclaimed, "We should dance while we sing."

More rehearsals ensued.

Finally all again were ready when, suddenly, Avery, the seven-year-old, decided she needed a musical instrument. She rushed into the kitchen, grabbed an empty coffee can and placing a small coconut in the can's empty center, created a resonant sounding bongo.

(May I interrupt the story to preach a little here?: These episodes of spontaneous creativity displayed by grandchildren suggest another difference between parents and renewed grandparents. From time to time, haven't we, as parents, experienced irritation when our children upset our schedule: "Wait!...Look at this. Wait!...See that." Hurrying, we fail to take time to see. Grandparents, most of the time, take time for looking and seeing. They have learned that waiting and watching bring unexpected pleasures when frenetic activity fills the hours. Let's all make time to see, really see, the people and things we love. Time spent paying attention, enjoying the moment and being thankful is time well spent.)

The bongo addition demanded more rehearsals. The bongo beat increased the children's enthusiastic singing and dancing, causing flowers to fall out of their hair and the leis to become tangled in their hands. The music stopped while the flowers were replaced and the costumes rearranged.

Finally, show time came! Just as the children were ready to open the door and begin the performance, Meagan shouted, "Hey, everybody — wait a minute! Remember, no matter what falls off just keep on dancing!"

As the children emerged from the room, singing and swinging, flowers fell off and leis became entangled — but they kept on dancing! The electrifying performance received a standing ovation and was recorded by three video cameras. (That's another difference between parents and grandparents. Grandparents always have cameras...and batteries.)

Inspired by Meagan's encouraging words, when things fell off, the children kept on singing and dancing. Little voices ringing. Bodies swaying. The coffee-can beating. Parents watching, laughing and loving. What a night! I was so elated, I passed the plate to receive an offering.

That time captured in the everlasting recesses of my mind, remains, always, a pleasure to recall. When I reflect on the swinging and swaying of that soft, sweet, summer night, Meagan's voice resounds in my mind's ear: "Hey everybody, wait a minute. Remember, no matter what falls off just keep on dancing."

Keep on dancing! What a magnificent prescription for life! We all know that along the exciting path of life's journey some things fall off. Nevertheless, no matter what falls off, we keep on dancing!

Keep on dancing, no matter what falls off!...and, to reverse the analogy, sometimes we must let things fall off to begin dancing. Some of us must remove impediments so we can dance joyfully, unfettered by past misfortunes.

As children we experience the shock of our toys tumbling, falling, and breaking. We didn't know that toys would break, until the first time we saw one shatter. An alarming number of children see their home life crumbling and breaking. They didn't know their home could break-up, until a parent leaves. Disappointments, losses, hurts, can come early in life producing emotional scars and sadness that, at times, persists through a lifetime of memories.

As we move down life's path, burdens — mistakes, setbacks, frustrations, and reversals — can weigh us down. Negative emotions engendered by misfortune impede our freedom so that we stagger though life. Dance? Some of us can't even walk.

Certain attitudes, practices, and habits formed from tragedies and calamities must fall off before we can begin to dance. May all of us who stumble and fall, whose life's burdens steal the joy of dance, be inspired by the words from *Hebrews 12:1*:

> *Therefore since we are surrounded by such*
> *a great crowd of witnesses,*
> *let us throw off everything that hinders*
> *and the sin that so easily entangles,*
> *and let us run with perseverance the race marked out for us.*

To run the race, to keep on dancing, we must rid ourselves of those burdens that pull us down, trip us up, paralyze our feet and turn us into lonely wallflowers standing in the corners of life watching everyone else dancing, laughing and enjoying life.

We don't need to look any further than our own experience to see some of the hindrances that have kept us from joyfully dancing. Having danced for years — beginning in junior high school — I learned early that if I were self-conscious and afraid to try, I would never be able to dance. I just had to "go for it" — regardless of whether I was good or not.

Self-centeredness only binds our feet. Preoccupation with self inevitably ties up life, destroys spontaneity and makes life clumsy, lonely and dreary.

Years later I discovered that religious legalism always paralyzes the muscles of our souls and destroys the joyful freedom essential to dancing to the exhilarating music of God's unconditional love and forgiveness.

The *Holy Bible* is both the most divine and human book in the world. Divine because the Bible introduces us to God and human because in the Bible's examples and warnings we see ourselves.

The Biblical characters are just like us. Their mistakes, sins, comforts, and joys are the same as ours.

Customs and dress change, but challenges and personalities remain the same through the ages. That's why the words in the Bible never grow old. The examples, warnings, and encouragements are as new today as they were 2000 years ago, because the challenges of confrontation and character are constant.

Consider the "Wallflower of Jericho" as recorded in *Mark 10:46-52*. His name, Bartimaeus, reveals the contempt society had for him. "Bar" is the Hebrew word for "son." This poor soul — a blind beggar — was simply called, "Son of Timaeus." His family, and the people of Jericho, looked upon him with such disdain that, as far as we know, he didn't even have a first name. He was a nothing. A nobody. A thing. The cruel world had turned his handicap into a nickname. "Blind" son of Timaeus. How horribly cruel!

It is important to remember that in Jesus' day any physical abnormality was looked upon by the self-righteous, ultra-religious crowd as being the result of sin — either individual sin or family sin. Jesus categorically and forcibly denied and rejected such an interpretation! According to Jesus, sin does not cause illness, although the consequences of sin may contribute to illness. For example, sin does not cause a person to develop diabetes mellitus, but the consequences of overeating (gluttony) would contribute to high blood sugar in a diabetic.

Unfortunately, the tendency to blame illness on sin or lack of faith is still with us. Even today, some Biblically misinformed individuals continue making the same hurtful and cruel accusations. Lack of faith does not cause illness. We don't know why some outstanding Christians die before their time.

We do know that "in all things God works for the good of those who love him" (*Romans 8:28*). And we do know — to repeat myself because the relationship of sin and disease is such a misunderstood concept — lack of faith does *not* cause illness. How do we know? Jesus said so (*John 9:1-41*). Perhaps understanding that you are not to blame for your illness or the illness of friends and loved ones will help you drop misinformed guilt so you can keep on dancing!

When "Blind" heard that Jesus was passing by, he cried out in desperation. The people in Jericho who thought his sins had caused his blindness told him to be quiet. "Keep your mouth shut," they said.

But he cried even louder. Why not? If you're already at the bottom of the pit, how can crying for help push you any lower?

"Jesus, son of David, have mercy on me," he cried.

At this point, we read one of the most startling verses in all the Bible. "Jesus stopped."

Think of that! The One who created the limitless universe — who set the stars and planets in perpetual motion, who scooped up the dust of the earth to make man, who began endless creativity — stopped in His tracks when a poor, neglected, rejected, blind beggar called His name! What a man! What a God! What a friend to us frightened and struggling companions seated beside Bartimaeus on the curbs of life wanting to see, to live, to dance.

Jesus startled the crowd when He suddenly said, "Call him."

A beautiful and tender scene follows. This poor, blind beggar, sitting helplessly beside the road, was suddenly invited to meet the Lord of life's dance. Jesus asked him what he wanted, and he cried, "Lord, that I might see."

Suddenly, Bartimaeus received his sight and "followed Jesus in the way."

What an incredible event! When the "Wallflower of Jericho" was invited to the dance of life, he was so excited, he "left his old coat beside the road."

His old coat, a symbol of a dark and desperate past, fell off when the Lord invited him to dance. His coat fell off as he followed Jesus and danced his way into life.

I can remember some of the things that began to fall off in my life when I, like Bartimaeus, called on Jesus and was invited to His dance. Upon going home to Dallas in 1946 after serving in the U.S. Marine Corps, I attended an evangelistic service and, in that meeting, "came home" to the Lord. I instantly saw some things begin to fall off — Marine expletives for one — and the more my colorful language fell, the lighter and happier I felt. After three-and-a-half years in a male world, I had accumulated quite a few inappropriate words that the Lord began to edit out of my life. My, how the Lord taught me to dance!

As we follow Christ, things begin falling off — not because of coercion, but because we feel the power of Jesus in our lives and are grateful for all He has done for us. We see joy and peace that comes from freeing ourselves from unreasonable guilt and burdens. Remember God wants us to be joyful. God wants us to dance!

Throughout church history, we read of devoted followers of the

Lord who experienced the loss of physical security, comfort, and safety; and yet, in spite of the loss of many things, they kept right on dancing.

The Apostle Paul's statement to the church in Corinth (*II Corinthians 4:1*), applies to each of us:

> *Therefore, since through God's mercy we have this ministry,*
> *we do not lose heart.*

He continues in *II Corinthians 6:4-7*:

> *Rather, as servants of God we commend ourselves in every way:*
> *in great endurance;*
> *in troubles, hardships and distresses;*
> *in beatings, imprisonments and riots;*
> *in hard work, sleepless nights and hunger;*
> *in purity, understanding, patience and kindness;*
> *in the Holy Spirit and in sincere love;*
> *in truthful speech and in the power of God;*
> *with weapons of righteousness in the right hand and in the left;...*

Paul continues (*II Corinthians 6:9b-10*):

> *dying, and yet we live on;*
> *beaten, and yet not killed;*
> *sorrowful, yet always rejoicing;*
> *poor, yet making many rich;*
> *having nothing, and yet possessing everything.*

He adds in *II Corinthians 4:7-9*:

> *But we have this treasure in jars of clay*
> *to show that this all-surpassing power is from God and not from us.*
> *We are hard pressed on every side, but not crushed;*
> *perplexed, but not in despair;*
> *persecuted, but not abandoned;*

struck down, but not destroyed.

In *II Corinthians 4:16-18*, Paul gives the reason for keeping our minds on the things that cannot be seen:

Therefore we do not lose heart.
Though outwardly we are wasting away,
yet inwardly we are being renewed day by day.
For our light and momentary troubles are achieving for us
an eternal glory that far outweighs them all.
So we fix our eyes not on what is seen, but on what is unseen.
For what is seen is temporary,
but what is unseen is eternal.

In his final written words, recorded in his second letter to *Timothy* (*4:6-8*), Paul triumphantly declares:

For I am already being poured out like a drink offering,
and the time has come for my departure.
I have fought the good fight,
I have finished the race,
I have kept the faith.
Now there is in store for me the crown of righteousness,
which the Lord, the righteous Judge, will award to me on that day —
and not only to me,
but also to all who have longed for His appearing.

In *II Timothy 4:17-18* Paul then concludes with a deeply moving statement:

But the Lord stood at my side and gave me strength,
so that through me the message might be fully proclaimed
and all the Gentiles might hear it.
And I was delivered from the lion's mouth.
The Lord will rescue me from every evil attack and will bring me safely

to his heavenly kingdom.
To Him be glory for ever and ever.
Amen.

Amen indeed! Today, using Meagan's words, Paul shouts to us across the centuries: "Hey everybody, wait a minute. No matter what falls off just keep on dancing!"

As Pastor of a wonderful congregation for over 40 years, I have witnessed countless people exemplify the same indomitable faith we see in the life of Paul. Sunday by Sunday, I look into the faces of thousands of dedicated people who have gone through the deep waters of adversity and emerged victorious. I see people who have lost their jobs, their health, their home, and their marriage. I hurt when I see victims of abuse and abandonment. The strong faces of victims of multiple sclerosis, muscular dystrophy and debilitating strokes face me each Sunday with smiling faces. Young children with cystic fibrosis sing in the choir. I watch families suffering with children on drugs or in jail singing *Amazing Grace* along with men and women who've "done time" in prison. I see many dear, wonderful Christian parents who have buried their children, and children who are praying for their parents. All kinds of people sing praises to the Lord Sunday by Sunday — businessmen and women who have experienced catastrophic bankruptcies sit together with others who are caring for severely handicapped children. As I look out at these victims of life's casualties, I fear my words fail to match the inspiration I feel coming from them.

These many people, whom I love so much, have kept on dancing the joyful and triumphant dance of faith, hope and love. Their lives are a divine witness to the sufficiency of God's under-girding, unfailing grace. There are thousands of these "angels masquerading around this planet as people," and my life is strengthened by each and all of them.

When interviewed a few years ago, I was asked what I felt was the major characteristic of the people I've pastored for over 40 years. Without hesitation I declared, "Christian courage!"

Countless Christians I know have confirmed again and again the great truth that we are "more than conquerors through Jesus Christ our Lord." We see thousands of God's angels masquerading as people doing and saying exactly what four-year-old Meagan announced, "Hey everybody, wait a minute! No matter what falls off, just keep on dancing."

Thank you, Meagan.

You're an angel!

BUCKNER FANNING: GOD'S SERVANT AROUND THE WORLD

Just about anyone with television access who has lived in South Texas for a few weeks knows of him. His 30-second TV spots seen nationally and twenty-eight times weekly in the San Antonio area make him easily recognizable. Pastor of Trinity Baptist Church in San Antonio since 1959 with four to five thousand in attendance each Sunday, and an active membership of over ten thousand, Dr. Buckner Fanning, is, in the words of Billy Graham, "the ideal pastor...a pastor evangelist whom God has greatly used."

After joining Trinity Baptist Church, which allowed me to appreciate the depth of Buckner's peace and joy, I, with hands clasped prayer-like, begged him to let me publish his next book. Buckner had become my pastor, mentor, and friend.

My desire to publish a book by Buckner Fanning was twofold. The first reason was selfish. Publishing a book of Buckner's would enable me to know more about him. The more insight I gained, the better man I would become. The second reason was altruistic. I wanted those who "know of" Dr. Buckner Fanning to know him as I have known him, and, in knowing, to be inspired toward love and good deeds.

Born in Houston in 1926, Buckner soon moved with his family to Dallas where his father was a claims manager for an insurance company. Buckner's parents, both dedicated Christians, shaped his life through their example of firm discipline balanced by love, patience, and understanding.

At the First Baptist Church in Dallas, Buckner was exposed to one of the most revered Baptist preachers of all time — Dr. George W. Truett — but to hear Buckner one gets the impression that, as a young man, he was less interested in singing in the choir than boxing or playing baseball and football.

Buckner graduated from Woodrow Wilson High School in 1943, and on his seventeenth birthday, enlisted in the U.S. Marine Corps. In the early autumn of 1945, the 19-year-old Marine, with the Second Division's Sixth Regiment, marched cautiously into Nagasaki.

Three weeks earlier, the world's second atomic bomb had scorched and flattened the city. The Nagasaki survivors, homeless and hungry, were haunted by memories of a tremendous flash, a searing wind, a cavernous boom...and silence. The infernal bludgeon killed over 35,000 people outright. Thousands others died later from burns and radiation sickness. The Nagasaki experience turned Buckner's glamorized war dreams into grisly memories of evil.

After three-and-a-half years in the Marine Corps, Buckner came home with vague ideas of going into the law. A revival meeting transformed him. Visions of his childhood combined with the nightmares of war, inspired Buckner to share his experience of God's regenerating love with others.

In recalling his Nagasaki experience, Buckner said, "We all have bombs fall in our lives — not all the scars show, but they're there. How does life come back after that? How do we find a way to turn suffering into something meaningful?"

God answered Buckner's search for meaning by calling him into the ministry. After graduating from Baylor in 1949 and from Fort Worth's Southwestern Baptist Theological Seminary in 1954, Reverend Fanning began receiving regular invitations to preach throughout the country.

In October, 1952, twenty-seven devout Texas businessmen formed the nonprofit Buckner Fanning Evangelistic Foundation to support Buckner's evangelistic efforts.

Newsweek, in the January 28, 1957, edition, gave Buckner, then 30 years old, his first national exposure with a two-column photograph and a two page article on his evangelistic efforts. *Newsweek* wrote that he was "warmhearted, up-to-date, and direct."

Buckner says his life became complete when, in 1949, he married Martha Howell. Martha, also a living legend, is a Southern Methodist University graduate, soprano soloist and artist. Martha's album, "The Lord Has Given Me A Song," sung with the Tokyo Symphony, received a "5-Star" rating by *Billboard Magazine.* She co-authored *What Every Woman Still Knows* with Mrs. Kenneth (Millie) Cooper and was named one of San Antonio's Ten Outstanding Women by the *San Antonio Express-News.* Martha speaks and sings for many organizations, both Christian and secular.

The deep, abiding love Martha and Buckner have for each other was blessed by their three children. Michael, a graduate of Baylor University and Southwestern Baptist Theological Seminar, has a Ph.D in Old Testament and Archaeology from Baylor. Having studied in Israel for two years, he is a pastoral consultant on Israeli travel. He and Buckner take many groups of both ministers and lay people to Israel. Over one thousand people have traveled with them.

Stephen, also a Baylor graduate, is a multimedia consultant and produces Buckner's televison ministries. He films, edits, and distributes the television films as well as providing many of the insights and ideas for the programs.

Lisa, a child psychology graduate of The University of Incarnate Word, works with children at risk in bereavement counseling. She is an assessment director and counselor in several children's homes.

The entire family enjoys contributing time and talent to the School at Mission Springs, an all inclusive Christian elementary school with emphasis on the fine arts and a classic education, established by the Buckner Fanning Evangelistic Foundation.

Of course, the lives of the Fanning's three children still excite Martha and Buckner as much as they once did, and those that know them recognize that their grandchildren are the joy of their lives! As do most grandparents, Martha and Buckner believe that their four grandchildren are more lovable than any of ours. They have photographs and stories to prove their contention — which they share with little or no solicitation.

There are not enough pages to list all of Buckner's accomplishments and honors. Here are just a few:

* Has preached in nearly every state and over 30 foreign countries

* Made fifteen evangelistic visits to Eastern Europe during the worst time of Communism

* Began Alpha Home — a rehabilitation home for women alcoholics — 30 years ago

* Produced several television specials seen nationally; one received the Gold Medal at the New York Television and Film Awards as the finest religious program of the year

* Selected by Religious Heritage of America as 1995 Clergyman of the Year

* Honorary Sergeant Major in U.S. Marine Corps

* Chaplain of the former Texas Rangers Association

* Recipient of the Outstanding Civilian Service Medal for the Department of the Army

* Selected by *Business Weekly* as one of the ten most influential persons in San Antonio

* Selected for Honorary Doctorates by The University of Incarnate Word and Howard Payne University

* Distinguished Alumnus award for Southwestern Baptist Theological Seminary

* On ten-member Board representing San Antonio at the "President's Summit for America's Future"

* Member of San Antonio Sports Foundation

* Spirit of Youth Award form Boys' Town of America

* Participated in countless Christian conferences, retreats and seminars

* Given motivational speeches to hundreds of secular or business and professional conventions and conferences

Honors and awards, though reflections of character, miss the depth and richness of a well lived life. Those of us privileged to call Buckner a friend — and there are many — have our individual impressions of his remarkable personality. Here are six traits that I think distinguish Buckner's character:

Joy filled. When Buckner enters the church, the congregation notices that this man is alive. The spring in his step tells us that he enjoys the opportunity to worship and praise. His broad beaming smile says, "I'm happy to see you." The twinkle in his eye lights the room. His *joi de vivre* energizes us all. Buckner, alone, is even more pleasing. In those times, his joy warms you, because you learn that happiness is not based on happenings, but on a calm, confident assurance of God's love for us all.

Peaceful. Buckner's verbal and nonverbal communication conveys contentment: His receptive face and tensionless body, seem to reflect the belief that God, the wise instructor, will help us discover the correct path for our lives if we learn to listen peacefully and patiently.

Magnanimous. Buckner is generous with praise and appreciative of the talents of others. His most frequently used words reflect this magnanimity: marvelous, incredible, extraordinary, remarkable.

Focused. Buckner is single-mindedly focused on preaching God's grace. Because Buckner focuses on God's word — The *Holy Bible* — he tells simple stories designed to give us a clear picture of God's love for all of us.

Humble. When my daughter first heard Buckner, she was impressed most with his sincerity and lack of pretension. Although Buckner has a powerful delivery, beautiful cadence, command for language, brilliant vocabulary, wonderful use of gestures, and an almost limitless supply of stories, historical accounts and quotations, his manner reverberates the importance of the message over the messenger.

Responsive. Buckner, open-minded and non-judgmental, cultivates friends from all faiths. Buckner, responsive to change, has painted a vision that will allow Trinity to minister to the inner city by the year 2000. He had one of the first audiotape and television ministries and has just launched a Web Site that will allow millions from around the world to hear and see his sermons as they are preached. Buckner, as any scholar, has developed a life-long pattern of continual education. One of his favorite quotes comes from Mark Twain: "The man who does not read good books has no advantage over the man who cannot read them."

To know Dr. Buckner Fanning is to appreciate a servant of God, a devoted husband and father, and a man who finds joy and purpose in his work. May his example — and the examples he has penned in this book — inspire all of us to lead more joyfilled, productive lives that glorify God.

John Ingram Walker, M.D.

The Mission of LifeWorks Publishing

To glorify God and enjoy Him forever by offering encouragement, inspiration, and hope to all we meet.

Specifically, we seek to make you laugh a little, think some, appreciate more, and, perhaps, on rare occasions, shed a tear or two.

We want you to know that LifeWorks when we work with God.

ORDER FORM

LifeWorks Publishing
7967 Turf Paradise Lane
Fair Oaks Ranch, Texas 78015
(210) 698-2758 / Fax: (210) 698-9158

QTY.	ITEM	UNIT	EXTENSION
	LEVERAGE YOUR TIME: BALANCE YOUR LIFE	Soft Cover: $15.00	
	A LIFE WELL LIVED	Soft Cover: $15.00	
	50 WAYS TO KEEP YOUR LOVER	Soft Cover: $10.00	
	JIM REID'S WINNING BASKETBALL	Soft Cover: $10.00	
	THE PEOPLE'S PSYCHIATRY: EVERYTHING YOU WANTED TO KNOW ABOUT YOURSELF (AND OTHERS) BUT WERE AFRAID TO ASK	Soft Cover: $19.95	
	GOD DRIVES A PICKUP TRUCK By Buckner Fanning	Soft Cover: $16.95	
	TOTAL SELF-HELP: THE FUNDAMENTAL PRINCIPALS OF PERSONAL GROWTH	Tape Series: $50.00	
	LIFE WORKS	One Year Subscription: $20.00	
		SUB-TOTAL:	
	TEXAS RESIDENTS: Add 7.75% Sales Tax:		
	Shipping & Handling: $3.50 per item		
		TOTAL ENCLOSED:	

PLEASE SHIP TO:

Name: _____

Mailing Address: _____

City, State and Zip: _____

Daytime Telephone: _____

❑ Please send information on presentations by LifeWorks speakers.

❑ Please send information on quantity discounts for the following title(s):

_____

_____

_____

_____

Since 1959, Buckner Fanning has been serving as Pastor of Trinity Baptist Church, San Antonio, Texas. His television, radio, audiocassette and Internet programs and his World-Wide evangelism confirm his reputation as "The Pastor of the Unchurched."

To learn more about Buckner Fanning and Trinity Baptist Church, go to www.trinitybaptist.org.

To hear audio recordings of the last few years of Buckner Fanning's sermons, go to www.thegospel.org.

'Tis the good reader that makes the good book; in every book he finds passages which seem confidences or asides hidden from all else and unmistakably meant for his ear; the profit of books is according to the sensibility of the reader; the profoundest thought or passion sleeps as in a mine, until it is discovered by an equal mind and heart.

Emerson